Incident reporting is a process that tracks and investigates incidents, this includes (1) a formal process for documenting incidents, including participants, materials and locations (2) tracking the events, actions and reasoning which led to the incident.

Artist Gabriel Hensche was in residence at La Cité Internationale des Arts, 18 rue de l'Hôtel de Ville, 75004 Paris, with the support of the State Ministry of Baden-Württemberg for Sciences, Research and Arts, Germany from November 1st 2016–July 9th 2017. Tethered to this stay, was an invitation to exhibit at The Foundation Centre Culturel Franco-Allemand Karlsruhe, as part of their series of exhibitions entitled *Retour-de-Paris*. A budget was given to mount an exhibition of the works that Hensche had produced during his time at La Cité, as well as the production of this publication.

The nature of the enclosed artworks (which are the material of this work), is to repeat themselves over days and months. This means they have accumulated numerous witnesses, some of whom even embodied them for a moment or two. Therefore no single expert exists on what will hereafter be referred to as 'incidents' rather than artworks. Adopting the posture of a Zuschauer [onlooker], even when acknowledging their role as Anstifter [instigator], contributing authors to this publication—Gabriel Hensche (artist) and Ashlee Conery (curator)—recount observations of these incidents; these are admittedly effected by events occurring within their own lives, Rückschaufehler [hindsight-bias], memory loss and personal expectations.

Gabriel Hensche, born 1986 in Dresden Germany, has been practicing with moving image, installation and performance for eight years. Having also participated in the Nida Art Colony (LT), Art Cube Artists' Studio Jerusalem (IL) and Viafarini, Milan (IT) residencies, his practice has implicated numerous other artists, curators, institutions and publics.

From Vancouver, Canada, Ashlee Conery is the Curatorial Interpreter at the Vancouver Art Gallery and a member of FormContent (London + Vienna).

| Co-authored: A.B. Conery, Gabriel Hensche | Graphic Design: Lukas Küng (Burrow, Berlin) |

Incident Title: *Like Father Like Son*
Date Incident Was Transferred To The Public: **May 25/17**
Environment In Which Incident Took Place: **Parisian apartment**

Category: **Performance**
Type Of Incident (Ex: Displacement, Collage, Analogy): **Constructed situation**
Media Affected/Effected (Ex: Canvas, Body, Objects): **Human bodies, photography**
Primary Impulse/Inspiration/Cause Of Incident (Ex: Encounter, Experience, Conversation): **Experience**

Name Of Person First Notified: **Estee Balsam**
Was A Relative Notified? **Yes**

Description of the event, including any obvious incident-related circumstances:

It happened during the exhibition *Jaqueline et Pierre,* which took place in a Parisian apartment. I included a little note in the exhibition's announcement asking visitors to bring their parents and grandparents, children and grandchildren—or any available family member—to the exhibition opening in the hope of gathering a group of visitors comprised of generations beyond the usual contemporary art audience. During the opening, I composed 'new families' by arranging people who did not know each other as if they were related and photographed them in a basic studio like set-up installed in the exhibition space. I was interested in the situation produced by the act of organizing and taking these photographs. How did these constructed family portraits—of families that existed only for the period of the camera's exposure—influence possible relations between participants? Did their roles within their own families simply transfer with them into their new families?

Like Father Like Son (2018) became the eponymous for my solo show at The Foundation Centre Culturel Franco-Allemand, where I installed these family portraits on the desks of CCFA employees instead of in the designated gallery space.

<table>
<tr><td colspan="2">

SECTION B: Incident Report

</td></tr>
<tr><td>

Supportive Measures Taken Prior To Incident
[Check All That Apply]:
- ☒ Increased level of observation
- ☒ Vivid cultural environment
- ☒ Artist integrated into the local art scene
- ☐ Professional group discussions

Motivation (mark appropriate):
enthusiasm obsession pleasure pain insomnia
struggle deadline Other: **My biography**

</td><td>

Functional Factors
[Check All That Apply]:
- ☒ Desire
- ☐ Loneliness
- ☒ Connectedness
- ☒ Electricity
- ☐ Food
- ☐ Drinks
- ☐ Emotional balance
- ☒ Emotional unbalance
- ☐ Other:

</td></tr>
<tr><td>

Cognitive Factors
[Check All That Apply]:
- ☒ Perception, attention
- ☒ Wondering
- ☐ Imagination, creativity
- ☒ Experimentation, play
- ☒ Planning, orientation
- ☐ Learning
- ☐ Memory
- ☐ Argumentation
- ☐ Introspection
- ☒ Extroversion
- ☐ Other:

</td><td>

Mobility
Position(s) taken (mark appropriate):
sitting standing lying moving rolling

Body part(s) involved (mark appropriate):
hands fingers arms eyes
ears head legs mouth toes
heart lungs hips Other:

</td></tr>
<tr><td rowspan="2">

**Environment(s) In Which The Incident
Was Conceived And/Or Executed**
[Answer with Yes or No]:
Studio **No**
Library **No**
Hardware store **Yes**
Workshops **No**
Space with adequate lighting **Yes**
Possibility for accommodation **Yes**

Acoustic environment (mark appropriate):
Music Noise Silence Other:
Cleanliness of environment (mark appropriate):
Clean Cluttered area Messy Other:
Recreational activities (mark appropriate):
Dancing Swimming Running Other:
Wifi (mark appropriate):
No connection Poor connection Good connection
Other:

</td><td>

Equipment Used To Manifest The Incident
[Check All That Apply]:
- ☐ Computer
- ☒ Chair
- ☐ Hot plate
- ☒ Camera
- ☐ Smartphone
- ☐ Projector
- ☐ Bicycle
- ☐ Bed
- ☒ Other:
**2×photo lamps, 2×reflectors,
flash, tripod**

</td></tr>
<tr><td>

Material Evidence With This Report
Mark Applicable Description(s) Of Accompanying
Material:

1st Page: Documentation Installation view
 Video Still Reproduction Other:

2nd Page: Documentation Installation view
 Video Still Reproduction Other:

3rd Page: Documentation Installation view
 Video Still Reproduction Other:

4th Page: Documentation Installation view
 Video Still Reproduction Other:

5th Page: Documentation Installation view
 Video Still Reproduction Other:
Opening speech by Didem Yazıcı, curator

</td></tr>
<tr><td>

Support
Name(s) And Function(s) Of The Person(s) Involved:
Laëtitia Striffling, light assistant

Assistant's Advice was useful? **Yes**
Needed More Advice That Was Not Available? **No**
Advice Safely Used By Affected Artist(s)? **No**
 Other:

</td><td></td></tr>
<tr><td>

Completed by Gabriel Hensche

</td><td>

Signature:

</td></tr>
</table>

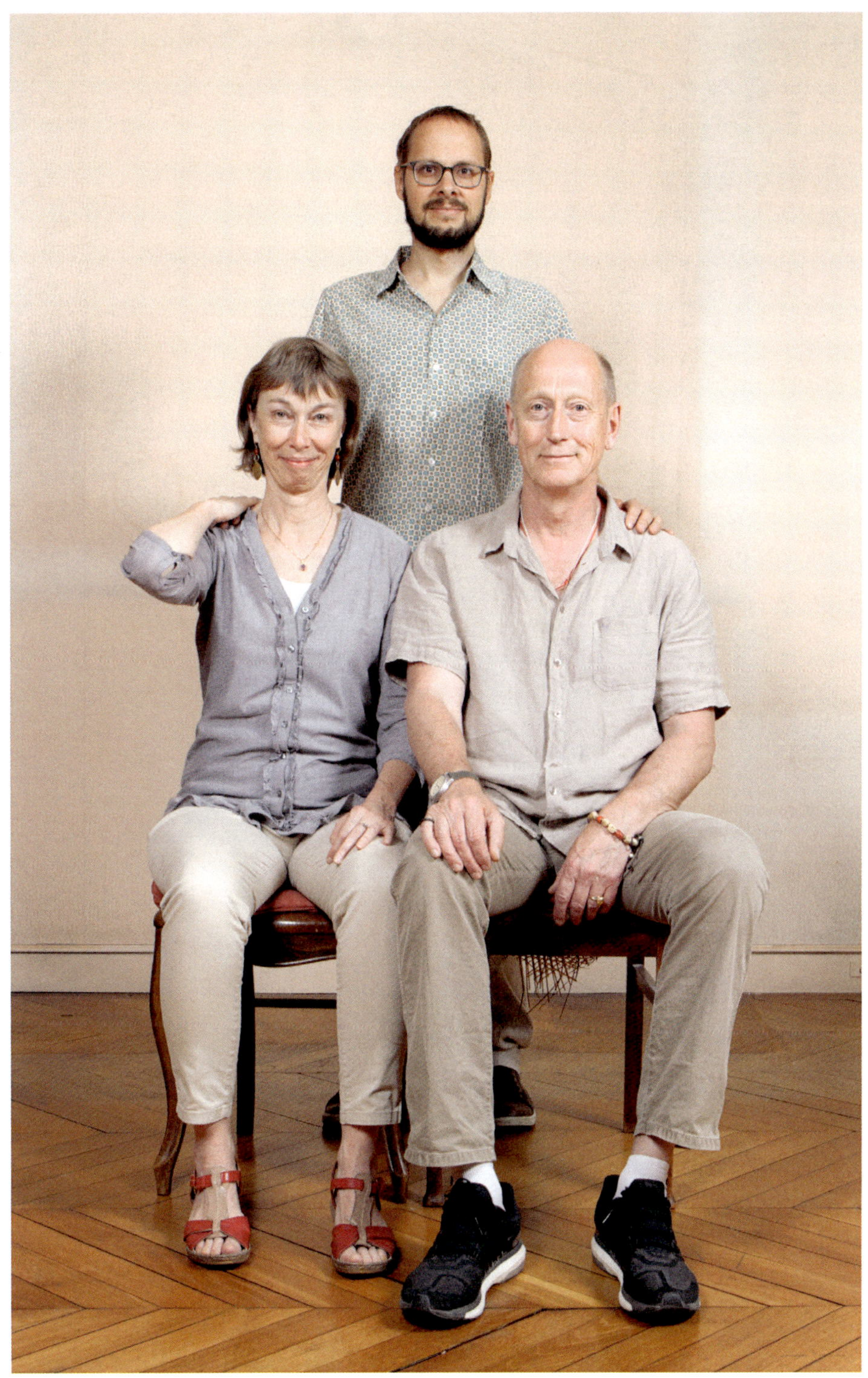

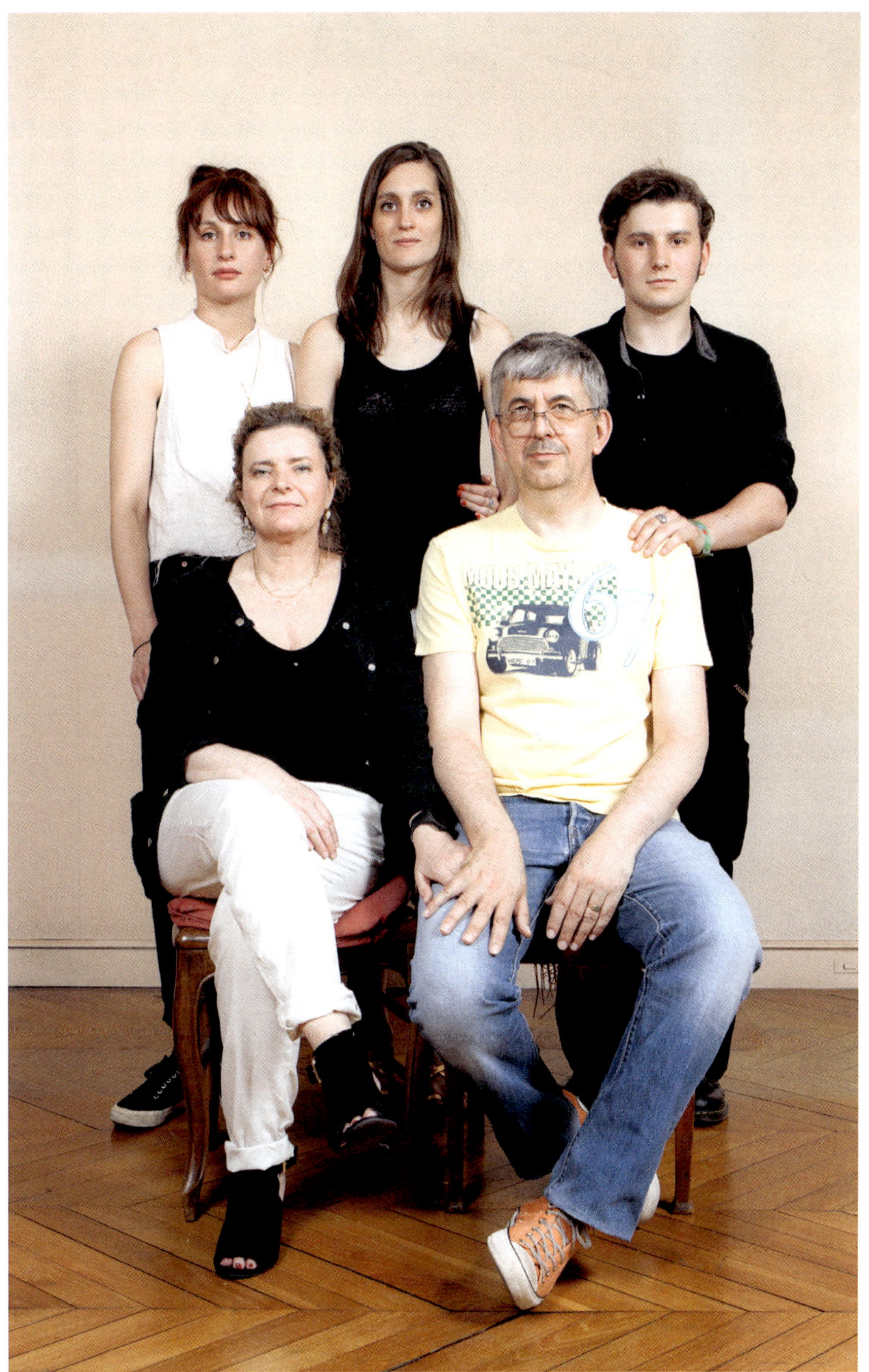

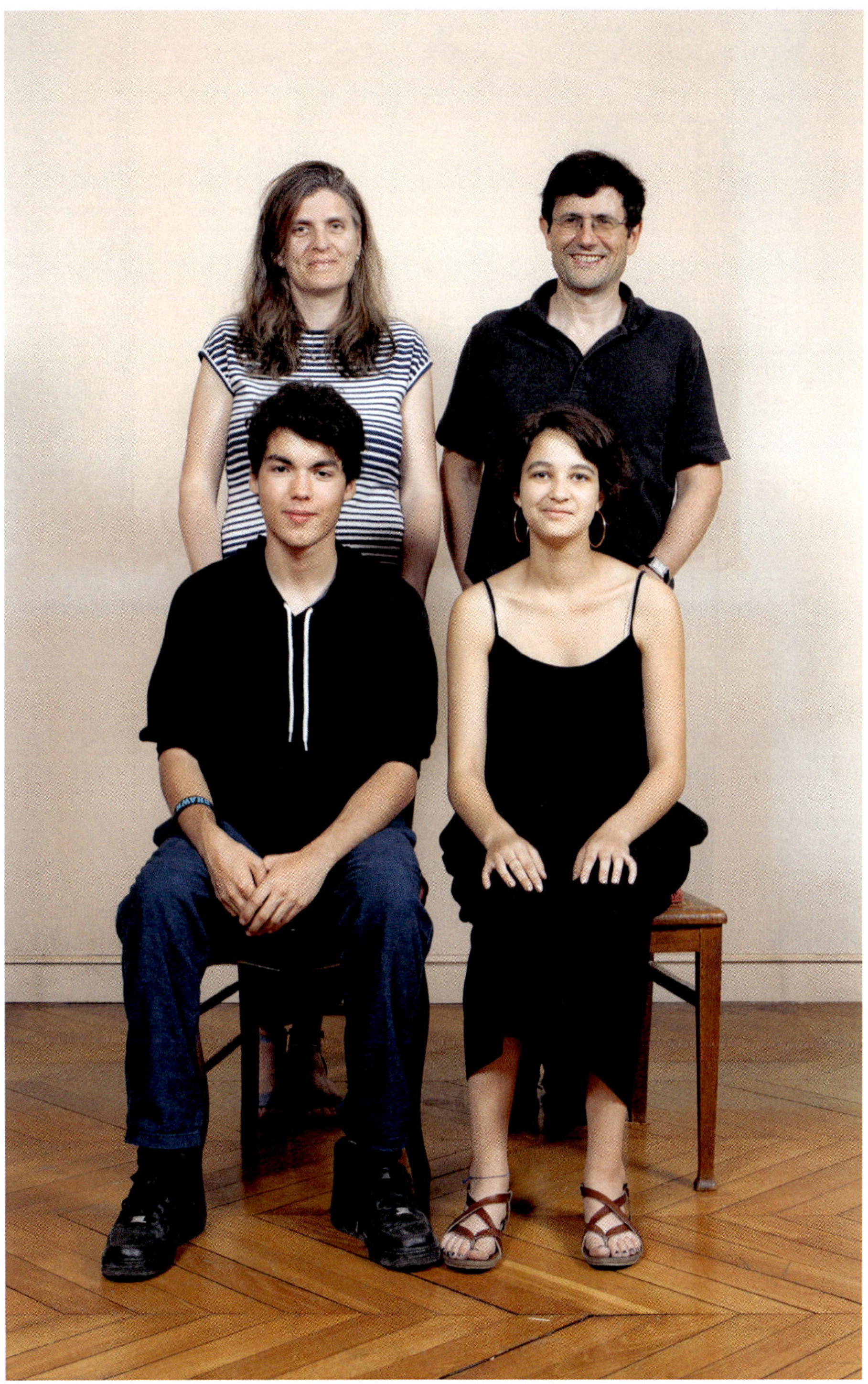

[handwritten, top:] → Morten Ryger! Thank you — and the ~~team~~ friendly team of Centre [?] Franco-Allemand for having me here!

Welcome everyone to
The solo presention of Gabriel Hensche:

I am not going to describe the art works that we are looking at tonight, but rather I would like to speculate on the spirit of these works and the discussion that they open:

Gabriel´s work is touching the issue that
very much about classical book – John Berger´s *Ways of Seeing*

"The relation between what we see and what we know is never settled. Each evening we see the sun set. We know that the earth is turning away from it. Yet the knowledge, the explanation, never quite fits the sight."
— **John Berger, Ways of Seeing**

I wanted start with this quote – because the exhibition´s background is very much about how we see things, how our interperations is based on our experiences, and how this information is produced in the world we live in today.

We belong to a generation that is living in the middle of **the ´Post-truth´condition**, and this is not just a problem of US. this is a problem of Europe, Middle East, Asia, Afrika. This is not a new problem, that we can no longer rely on information that is mediated through television, internet, newspapers.

The world we live in today, information on the main stream media is not reliable.

New technologies incresingly became part of our everday life realitues, it is used in military context, football, statistics, politics, the way we live, the way we experience, see and understand things.

[handwritten margin: why we started here]

We often find ourselves, saying „I AM NOT SURE" – because, we constantly need to check the validity of this information. I will open 4 brackets here ~~and~~ say: According to the lens of an **application for blinds, which is the main element in the video piece,** or just our inner justice senses; a naked woman can be read as swimwear, a real apple can be read as macinthos apple, OR European Unions Immigration policy can be in reality actually be more dangerous than actual far-right politics. We are just not SURE!! Unless we push ourselves to the dedication for transparency, justice and sincerity of artistic freedom.

[handwritten margin: Maybe we're all looking at more than blind]

Now, looking at Gabriel´s body of work:
He is an artist who is deeply interested in commenting on things that are in constant FLUX, ~~things~~ things that are not static, like **FAMILIES** How do we connect to one another, how do we connect to a stranger? How does it feel, when you form a temporary family at an exhibition opening? What if we imagine we are a one big family right now?

[handwritten:] Gabriel is an artist who doesn't take things as it is.

In his exhibition in Paris, he included a little note in the annoucenment: asking the audience bring their parents, grandparents, children, or grandchildren or any other family members to the exhibition opening. Hoping that he could gather a cross-generational audience beyond the usual contemporary art followers.

During the opening, he composed NEW families out of the audience right at evening on that moment like a temporary patchwork way.

Gabriel plays with the standard, traditional hetero-normative understanding of a family. He asks „ How do these newly constructed fanilies – that exists only for the moment of the camera´s shitter speed – influence the reltion between its members?"

BUT, there is actually more than that. It is not only about the temporary connection and familiar feeling that is quickly built at the moment. It´s also about the social and psychological conditions around it. First impressions that you gez while meeting a new person. Psychologists call it "thin slicing." Within seconds of meeting you, people decide all sorts of things about you. According to scientific studies, I will highlight just how important a first impression can be.

There are 8 things that people decide within seconds when meeting a stranger:

1) If you are trust-worthy person or not
2) If you are high status, mostly depending on your apperance, it can be cloth you are wearing, it can be the color of your skin tone, your accent.
3) If you are gay or not
4) If you are smart
5) If you are successful
6) If you are dominant
7) If you are immoral (according to stereotypes,people perceive women with visible tattooes as less attractive, heavy drinkers)
8) If you're adventurous.

These stereotypical codes are deeply rooted in conservative and heteronormative subsconsciousness.

Gabriel´s work: Like Father, Like Son – is also Like Mother, Like Daugther, Like Her, Like Him – it is an experiment on breaking the boundaries when we touch, look in eye or develop a friendship and familiarity among us.

The world needs more human connection, more trust, more compassion, more collectivity, more friendship. I would like say THANK YOU to Gabriel to open up s pace that allows us to speak about the feelings and concepzs that matter which is very abstract and experi

And the send well - puts you directly in the situation - of ~~Doubt~~ or here you doubt about the given information

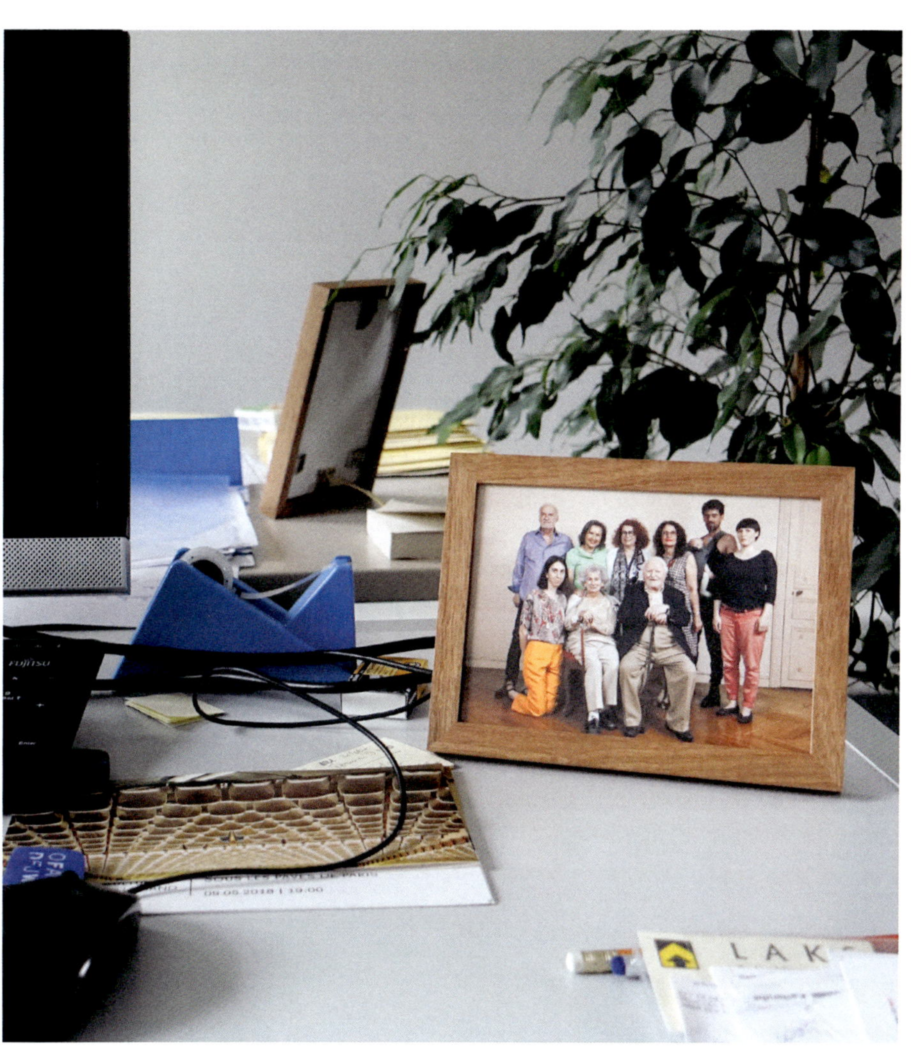

Incident Title: *It Felt Like Walking Into The TV*
Date Incident Was Transferred To The Public: **December 2/17**
Environment In Which Incident Took Place: **Public space/galerie l'inlassable**

Category: **Audio walk**
Type Of Incident (Ex: Displacement, Collage, Analogy): **Inadequate use**
Media Affected/Effected (Ex: Canvas, Body, Objects): **Human bodies, audio**
Primary Impulse/Inspiration/Cause Of Incident (Ex: Encounter, Experience, Conversation): **Experience**

Name Of Person First Notified: **Sascha Brosamer**
Was A Relative Notified? **Yes**

Description of the event, including any obvious incident-related circumstances:

I invited visitors to go for a walk through galerie l'inlassable's neighbourhood in Paris. They were given headphones with built-in microphones, attached to smartphones, which navigated them through space and time. The GPS system would tell them where they were in the present while listening to the past—a soundscape of that same path taken during the previous visitors walk. During their own journey the microphone would continue this cycle, recording the present soundscape for future walkers. Therefore, in undertaking this walk they became producers and simultaneously witnesses of the previous walkers experience. While walking, I wondered how we can experience a given moment in a recorded world?

SECTION B: Incident Report

Supportive Measures Taken Prior To Incident

[Check All That Apply]:
- ☒ Increased level of observation
- ☒ Vivid cultural environment
- ☒ Artist integrated into the local art scene
- ☐ Professional group discussions

Motivation (mark appropriate):
  |enthusiasm| obsession |pleasure| pain insomnia
  struggle |deadline| Other:

Cognitive Factors

[Check All That Apply]:
- ☒ Perception, attention
- ☐ Wondering
- ☐ Imagination, creativity
- ☐ Experimentation, play
- ☐ Planning, orientation
- ☒ Learning
- ☐ Memory
- ☐ Argumentation
- ☒ Introspection
- ☐ Extroversion
- ☐ Other:

Environment(s) In Which The Incident Was Conceived And/Or Executed

[Answer with Yes or No]:
Studio **No**
Library **Yes**
Hardware store **Yes**
Workshops **No**
Space with adequate lighting **Yes**
Possibility for accommodation **Yes**

Acoustic environment (mark appropriate):
  Music |Noise| Silence Other:
Cleanliness of environment (mark appropriate):
  Clean |Cluttered area| Messy Other:
Recreational activities (mark appropriate):
  |Dancing| Swimming |Running| Other:
Wifi (mark appropriate):
  No connection |Poor connection| Good connection
  |Other:| **Personal Hotspot**

Support

Name(s) And Function(s) Of The Person(s) Involved:
Employees of different electronics stores

Assistant's Advice was useful? **No**
Needed More Advice That Was Not Available? **Yes**
Advice Safely Used By Affected Artist(s)? **No**
  Other:

Functional Factors

[Check All That Apply]:
- ☒ Desire
- ☒ Loneliness
- ☐ Connectedness
- ☒ Electricity
- ☐ Food
- ☐ Drinks
- ☐ Emotional balance
- ☒ Emotional unbalance
- ☐ Other:

Mobility

Position(s) taken (mark appropriate):
  sitting standing lying |moving| rolling

Body part(s) involved (mark appropriate):
  hands fingers arms eyes
  |ears||head||legs| mouth toes
  heart |lungs| hips Other:

Equipment Used To Manifest The Incident

[Check All That Apply]:
- ☐ Computer
- ☐ Chair
- ☐ Hot plate
- ☐ Camera
- ☒ Smartphone
- ☐ Projector
- ☐ Bicycle
- ☐ Bed
- ☒ Other: **Binaural microphones/earphones**

Material Evidence With This Report

Mark Applicable Description(s) Of Accompanying Material:

1st Page: |Documentation| Installation view
           Video Still Reproduction Other:

2nd Page: Documentation Installation view
           Video Still Reproduction |Other:|
           Transcript of a visitor's account/route

3rd Page: Documentation Installation view
           Video Still Reproduction Other:

4th Page: Documentation Installation view
           Video Still Reproduction Other:

5th Page: Documentation Installation view
           Video Still Reproduction Other:

Completed by Gabriel Hensche	**Signature:**

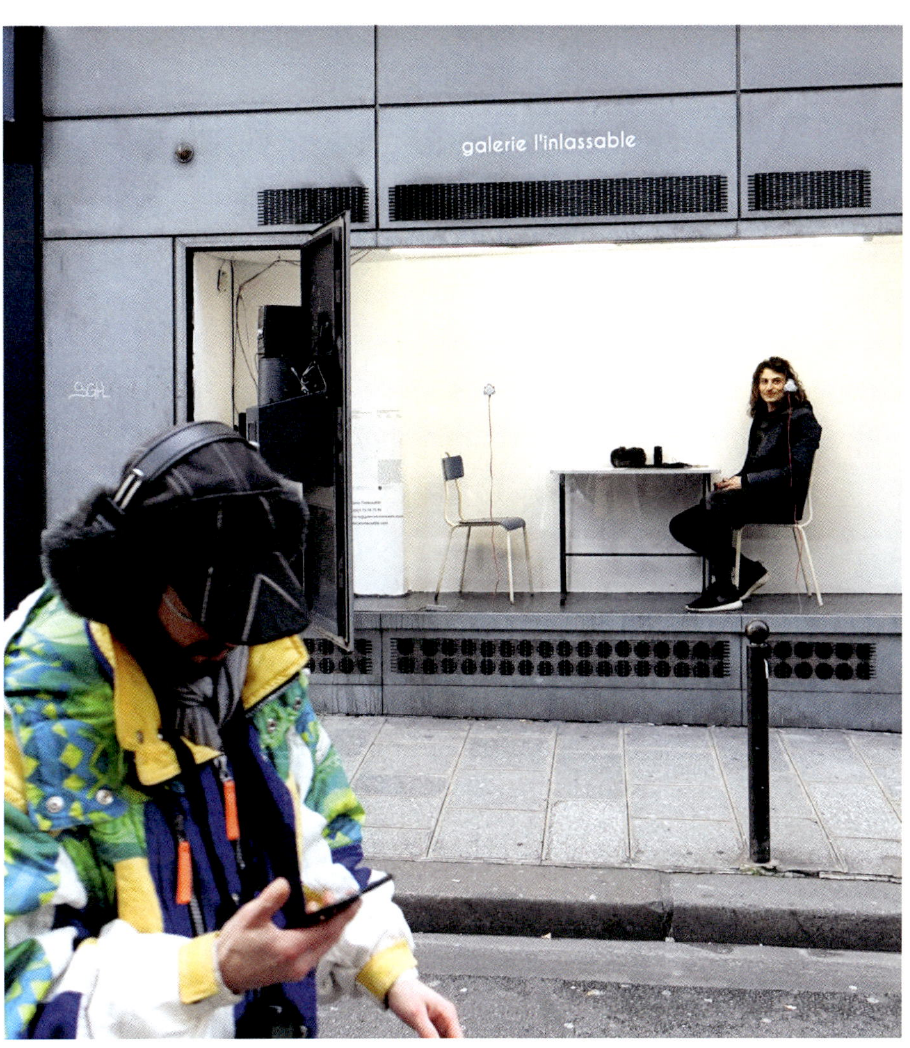

galerie l'inlassable

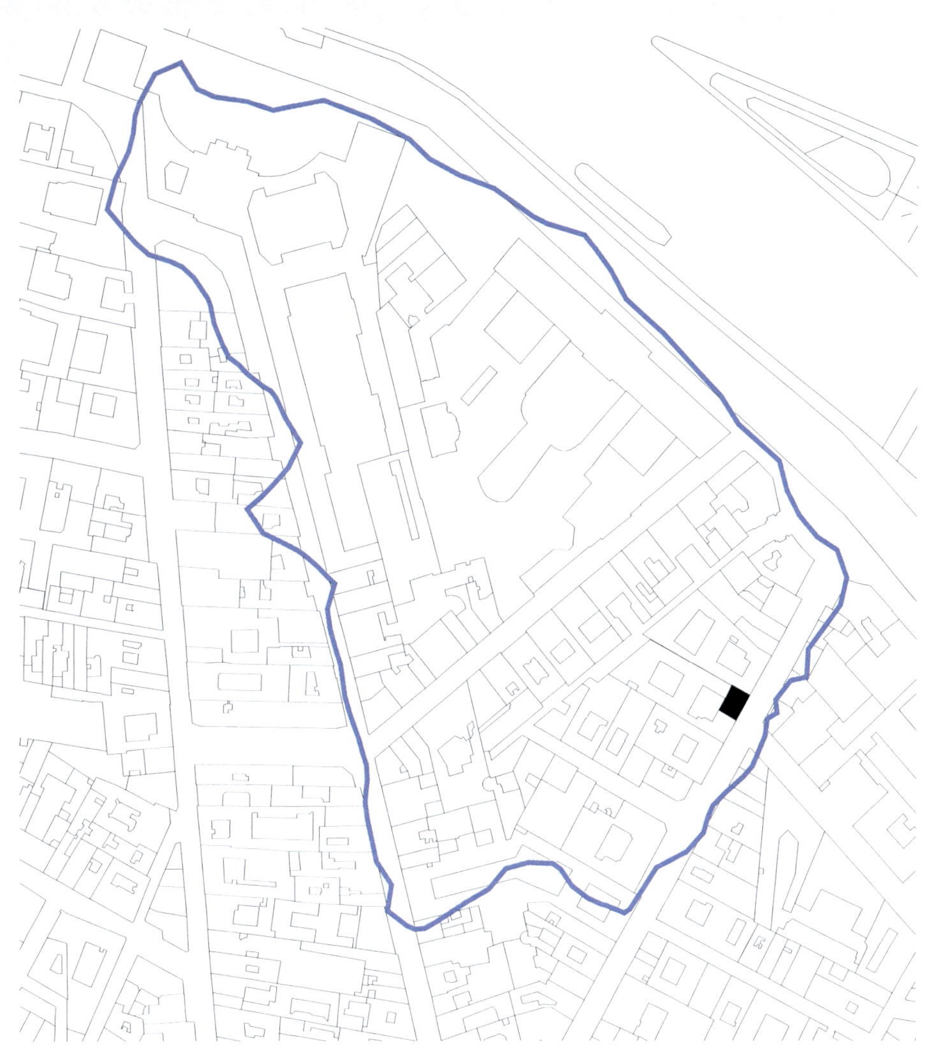

"At first, everything sounds like what I'm seeing and then suddenly, there was no traffic and then I was afraid because I heard the scooters and I was like—you can probably hear me saying 'shit, what the fuck'. And sometimes I hear someone is following me but maybe it is the recording of someone else, and I was looking behind me to see, and there was this old lady—but it's not her, I know it's not her [...]."

Incident Title: *Closed Studio*   Feb 2, 6, 13, 20, 27/17 Mar 6, 13, 20, 27/17
Date Incident Was Transferred To The Public: Apr 3, 10, 17, 20/17 May 3, 10, 17, 24/17 Jun 5, 12/17
Environment In Which Incident Took Place: Studio (No. Q 2051), Cité Internationale des Arts

Category: Social space
Type Of Incident (Ex: Displacement, Collage, Analogy): Constructed situation
Media Affected/Effected (Ex: Canvas, Body, Objects): Various artistic practices
Primary Impulse/Inspiration/Cause Of Incident (Ex: Encounter, Experience, Conversation): Encounter

Name Of Person First Notified: Several artists were invited simultaneously
Was A Relative Notified? Yes

Description of the event, including any obvious incident-related circumstances:

La Cité Internationale des Arts hosts more than 300 artists from all around the world, housing most of them in one of three buildings. I found myself in this utopian world, where everybody is an artist. While in wonder of it, I also felt that we, the Cité artist's, were like astronauts who had landed in one of Paris' richest areas. I became interested in the other astronauts and started to go to their Open Studios. In doing so I realized we were performing standard procedures for getting to know each other. These encounters always started with questions like: "What is your name? Where are you from? How long are you here? Why are you here?". I tried to create new opportunities for connecting by organizing *Closed Studios.* These comprised of a group of artists from the Cité (who didn't know each other), meeting with a small set of rules: each artist was asked to show/perform a part of their work; after their presentation the other artists were asked to discuss the presented work; and throughout the discussion the artist who presented was not allowed to explain their work or respond to questions, they could only listen. As the first meeting ended with a common wish for continuation, I decided to Close my Studio every week for these gatherings. Soon they became part of my artistic investigations, causing me to reflect on basic questions like, how an artist residency influences art practices.

Artists implicated in incident: Stéphanie Baechler, Aziyadé Baudouin-Talec, Sascha Brosamer, Osmar Domingos, Sophie Dupont, Simone Etter, Rotem Gerstel, Laura Gozlan, Sarah Haddou, Klara Hobza, Anita Holtsclaw, Sophie Innmann, Claudia Kübler, Johan Lundin, Nourhan Maayouf, France Manoush Sahatdjian, Anna McMahon, Petra Mrša, Paulien Oltheten, Christoph Poetsch, Eden Sarna, Goran Škofić, Laëtitia Striffling, Akira Takaishi, Lauren Tortil, Nicholas Vargelis, Riki Werdenigg, Julia Wirsching and others

Supportive Measures Taken Prior To Incident

[Check All That Apply]:
- ☒ Increased level of observation
- ☒ Vivid cultural environment
- ☐ Artist integrated into the local art scene
- ☐ Professional group discussions

Motivation (mark appropriate):
|enthusiasm| obsession |pleasure| pain insomnia
|struggle| deadline Other:

Cognitive Factors

[Check All That Apply]:
- ☒ Perception, attention
- ☐ Wondering
- ☐ Imagination, creativity
- ☐ Experimentation, play
- ☒ Planning, orientation
- ☒ Learning
- ☐ Memory
- ☒ Argumentation
- ☐ Introspection
- ☒ Extroversion
- ☒ Other: **Curiosity**

Environment(s) In Which The Incident Was Conceived And/Or Executed

(Answer with Yes or No):
Studio **Yes**
Library **No**
Hardware store **No**
Workshops **No**
Space with adequate lighting **Yes**
Possibility for accommodation **Yes**

Acoustic environment (mark appropriate):
|Music| Noise |Silence| Other:
Cleanliness of environment (mark appropriate):
|Clean| Cluttered area Messy Other:
Recreational activities (mark appropriate):
|Dancing| Swimming Running Other:
Wifi (mark appropriate):
No connection |Poor connection| Good connection
Other:

Support

Name(s) And Function(s) Of The Person(s) Involved:
All artists mentioned above participated by sharing and discussing work

Assistant's Advice was useful?
Needed More Advice That Was Not Available?
Advice Safely Used By Affected Artist(s)?
Other:

Functional Factors

[Check All That Apply]:
- ☒ Desire
- ☐ Loneliness
- ☒ Connectedness
- ☒ Electricity
- ☒ Food
- ☒ Drinks
- ☒ Emotional balance
- ☐ Emotional unbalance
- ☐ Other:

Mobility

Position(s) taken (mark appropriate):
|sitting| |standing| lying |moving| |rolling|

Body part(s) involved (mark appropriate):
|hands| |fingers| |arms| |eyes|
|ears| |head| |legs| |mouth| toes
heart lungs |hips| Other:

Equipment Used To Manifest The Incident

[Check All That Apply]:
- ☒ Computer
- ☒ Chair
- ☒ Hot plate
- ☐ Camera
- ☒ Smartphone
- ☒ Projector
- ☐ Bicycle
- ☐ Bed
- ☒ Other: **Extra chairs and drinking glasses**

Material Evidence With This Report

Mark Applicable Description(s) Of Accompanying Material:

1st Page: |Documentation| Installation view
Video Still Reproduction Other:

2nd Page: |Documentation| Installation view
Video Still Reproduction Other:

3rd Page: Documentation Installation view
Video Still Reproduction Other:

4th Page: Documentation Installation view
Video Still Reproduction Other:

5th Page: Documentation Installation view
Video Still Reproduction Other:

Completed by Gabriel Hensche | **Signature:**

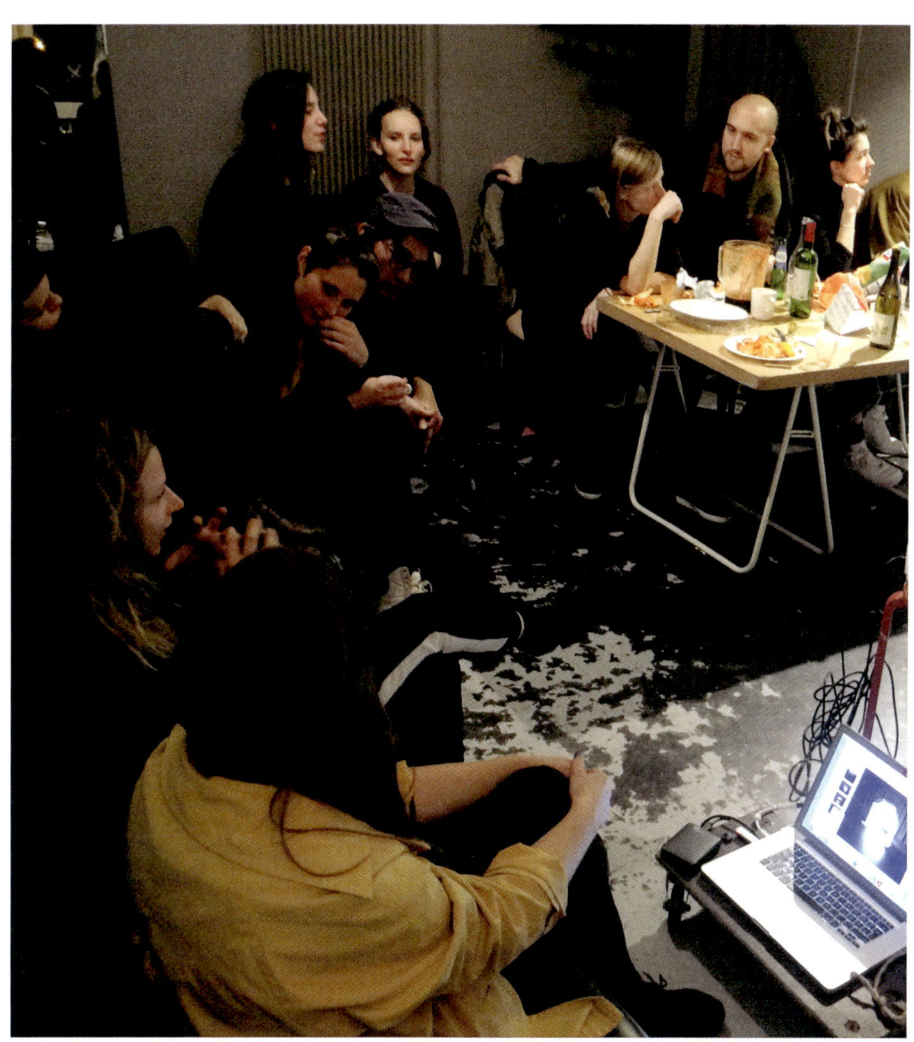

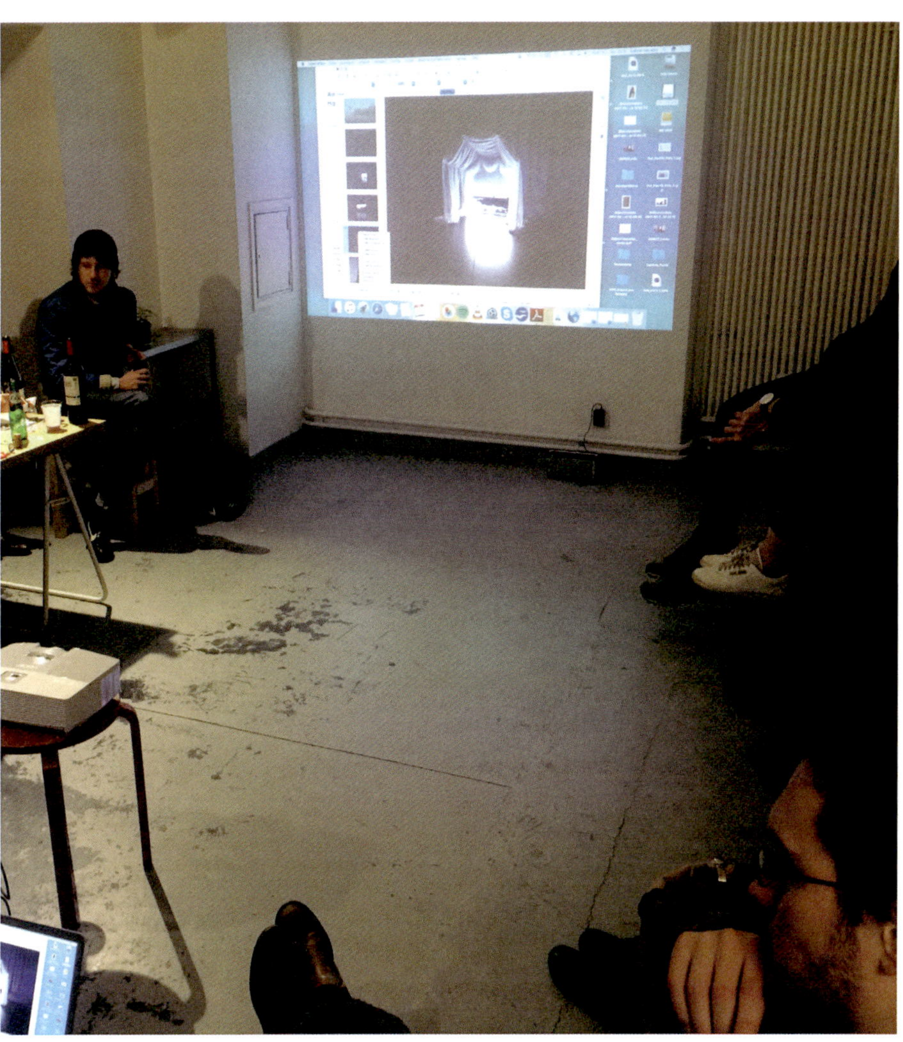

Incident Title:*I'm Not Sure*
Date Incident Was Transferred To The Public:Jan 20/18
Environment In Which Incident Took Place:Slamdance Film Festival, Park City

Category:Experimental short film
Type Of Incident (Ex: Displacement, Collage, Analogy):Inadequate use
Media Affected/Effected (Ex: Canvas, Body, Objects):Moving image
Primary Impulse/Inspiration/Cause Of Incident (Ex: Encounter, Experience, Conversation):Experiment

Name Of Person First Notified:Maximilian Eber
Was A Relative Notified?Yes

Description of the event, including any obvious incident-related circumstances:

The film *I'm Not Sure* shows how an app, designed to be a vision-aid for the visually impaired, interprets art. By confronting the Neural Image Caption Generator with surrealist paintings, *I'm Not Sure* explores the psychology of artificial intelligence. As I used an iPad to record *I'm Not Sure,* artificial intelligence was not only operating the image caption generator, but less obviously, the camera. In contrast to traditional cameras, this device (like all smartphones) uses computational photography. Half of the data that is captured by the tiny iPad lens is noise, which means the picture we see is calculated by an algorithm that creates the picture based on pictures it's taken previously. This means that most of today's images are produced from the data stored in our technology rather than a process of transposing reflections. Hence, *I'm Not Sure* is not only a dialogue between art and technology, but a conversation between devices.

Like an infant, artificial intelligence needs to learn, furthermore it needs a lot of input data in order to become intelligent. While watching *I'm Not Sure* guessing, I wondered how its algorithm was programmed and what kind of pictures were used to train it. Who decides and for what reasons, which data is relevant, and what is just noise? Why does the algorithm say "swimwear" while seeing Rene Margerite's painting of a naked woman? Is it too shy to say "breast", "butt" or "vagina"? Perhaps it has mainly been exposed to product pictures and was rarely introduced to art?

<table>
<tr><td colspan="2">SECTION B: Incident Report</td></tr>
<tr><td>

Supportive Measures Taken Prior To Incident
[Check All That Apply]:
☒ Increased level of observation
☐ Vivid cultural environment
☐ Artist integrated into the local art scene
☐ Professional group discussions
Motivation (mark appropriate):
  |enthusiasm| obsession pleasure pain insomnia
  |struggle| deadline Other:

Cognitive Factors
[Check All That Apply]:
☒ Perception, attention
☒ Wondering
☐ Imagination, creativity
☒ Experimentation, play
☐ Planning, orientation
☒ Learning
☐ Memory
☐ Argumentation
☐ Introspection
☐ Extroversion
☐ Other:

Environment(s) In Which The Incident
Was Conceived And/Or Executed
[Answer with Yes or No]:
Studio **Yes**
Library **No**
Hardware store **No**
Workshops **No**
Space with adequate lighting **Yes**
Possibility for accommodation **Yes**

Acoustic environment (mark appropriate):
  Music |Noise| Silence Other:
Cleanliness of environment (mark appropriate):
  |Clean| Cluttered area Messy Other:
Recreational activities (mark appropriate):
  |Dancing| Swimming Running Other:
Wifi (mark appropriate):
  No connection Poor connection |Good connection|
  |Other:| **Centre Pompidou,**
          Magritte exhibition

Support
Name(s) And Function(s) Of The Person(s) Involved:
Jela Hasler, editing advisor
Julia Wirsching, lent me her iPad
Sophie Inmann, lent me her camera

Assistant's Advice was useful? **Yes**
Needed More Advice That Was Not Available? **No**
Advice Safely Used By Affected Artist(s)? **Yes**
  Other:

</td><td>

Functional Factors
[Check All That Apply]:
☒ Desire
☒ Loneliness
☐ Connectedness
☒ Electricity
☐ Food
☐ Drinks
☐ Emotional balance
☒ Emotional unbalance
☐ Other:

Mobility
Position(s) taken (mark appropriate):
  |sitting| standing lying |moving| rolling

Body part(s) involved (mark appropriate):
  hands |fingers| arms |eyes|
  |ears| head legs mouth toes
  heart lungs hips Other:

Equipment Used To Manifest The Incident
[Check All That Apply]:
☒ Computer
☒ Chair
☐ Hot plate
☒ Camera
☐ Smartphone
☐ Projector
☐ Bicycle
☐ Bed
☒ Other:
iPad, Aipoly vision app

Material Evidence With This Report
Mark Applicable Description(s) Of Accompanying
Material:

1st Page: Documentation Installation view
            |Video Still| Reproduction Other:

2nd Page: Documentation Installation view
            |Video Still| Reproduction Other:

3rd Page: Documentation Installation view
            |Video Still| Reproduction Other:

4th Page: Documentation Installation view
            |Video Still| Reproduction Other:

5th Page: Documentation Installation view
            |Video Still| Reproduction Other:

</td></tr>
<tr><td>Completed by Gabriel Hensche</td><td>Signature:</td></tr>
</table>

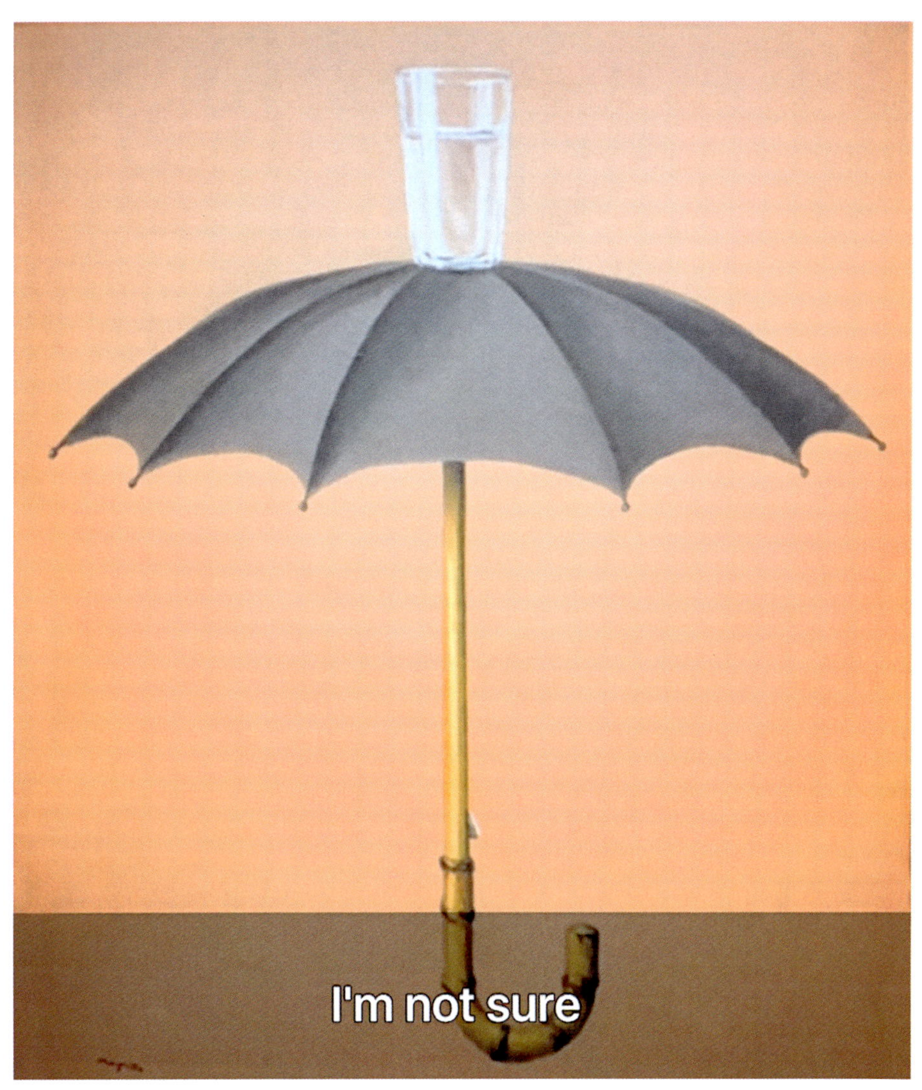

I'm not sure

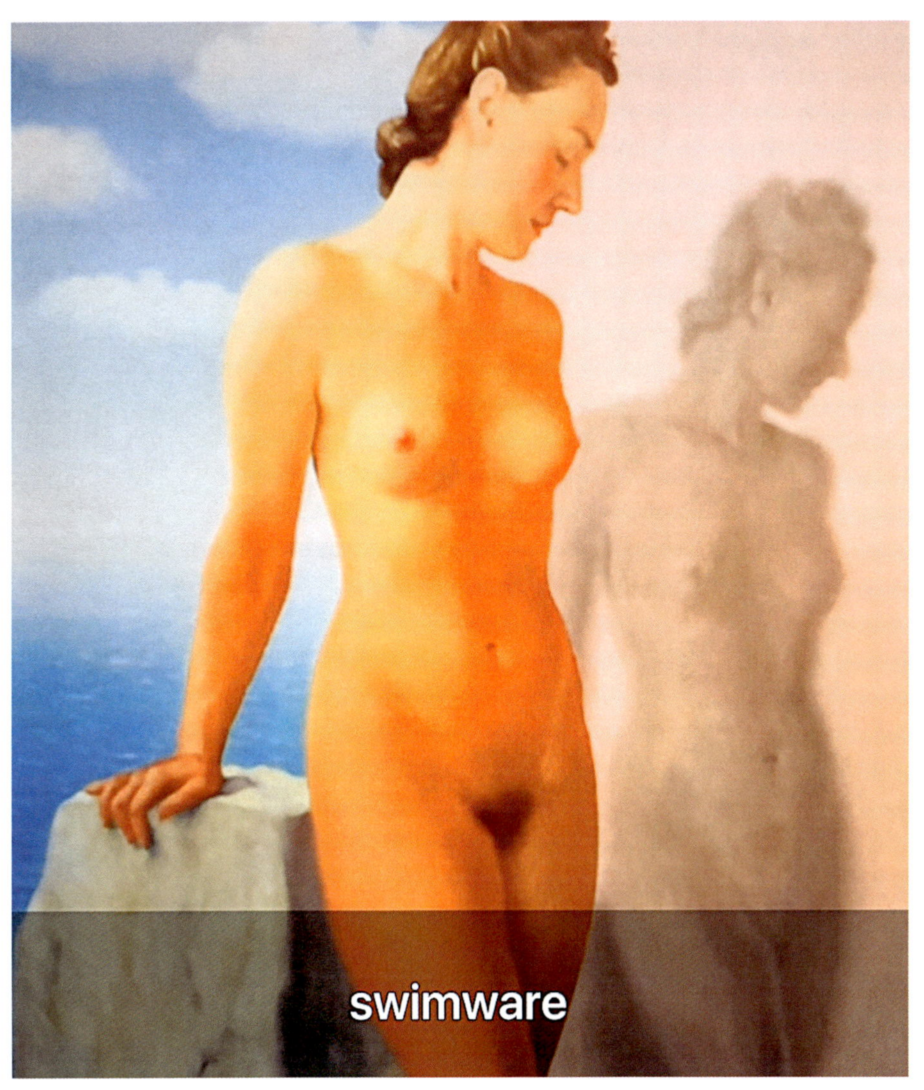

swimware

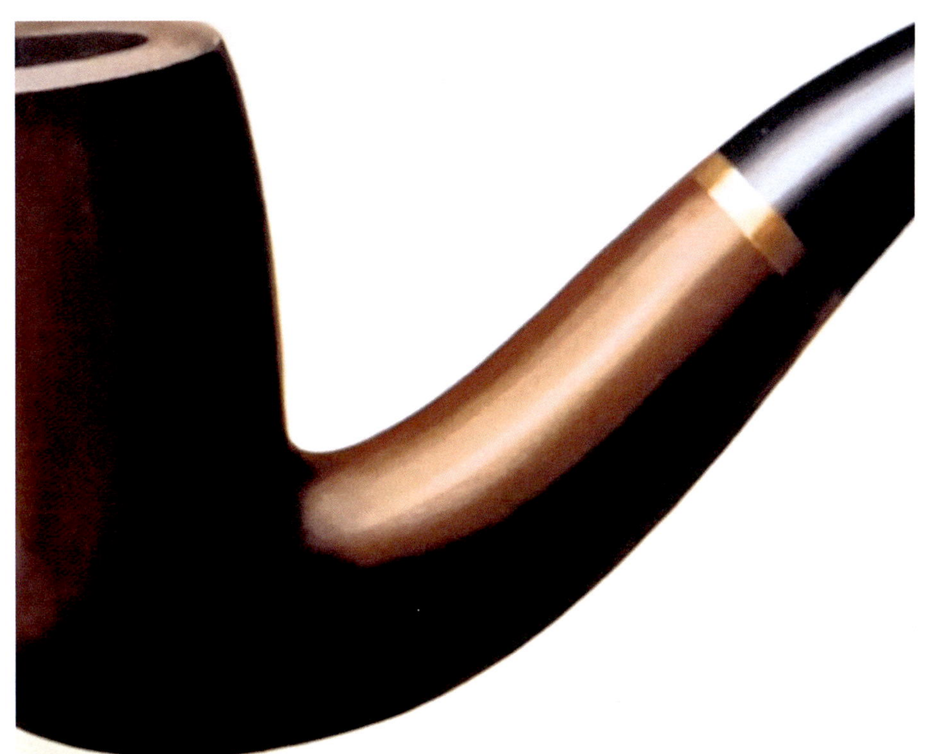
Ceci n'est pas un
I'm not sure

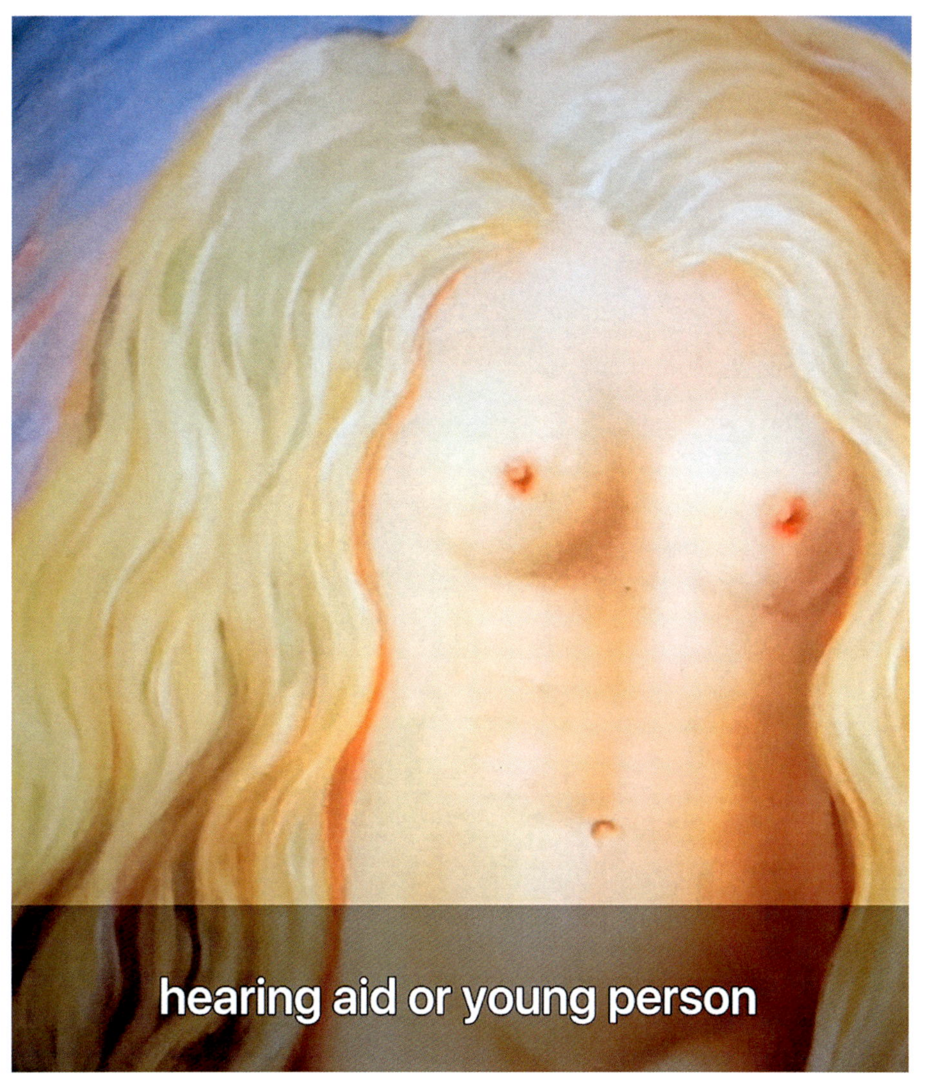
hearing aid or young person

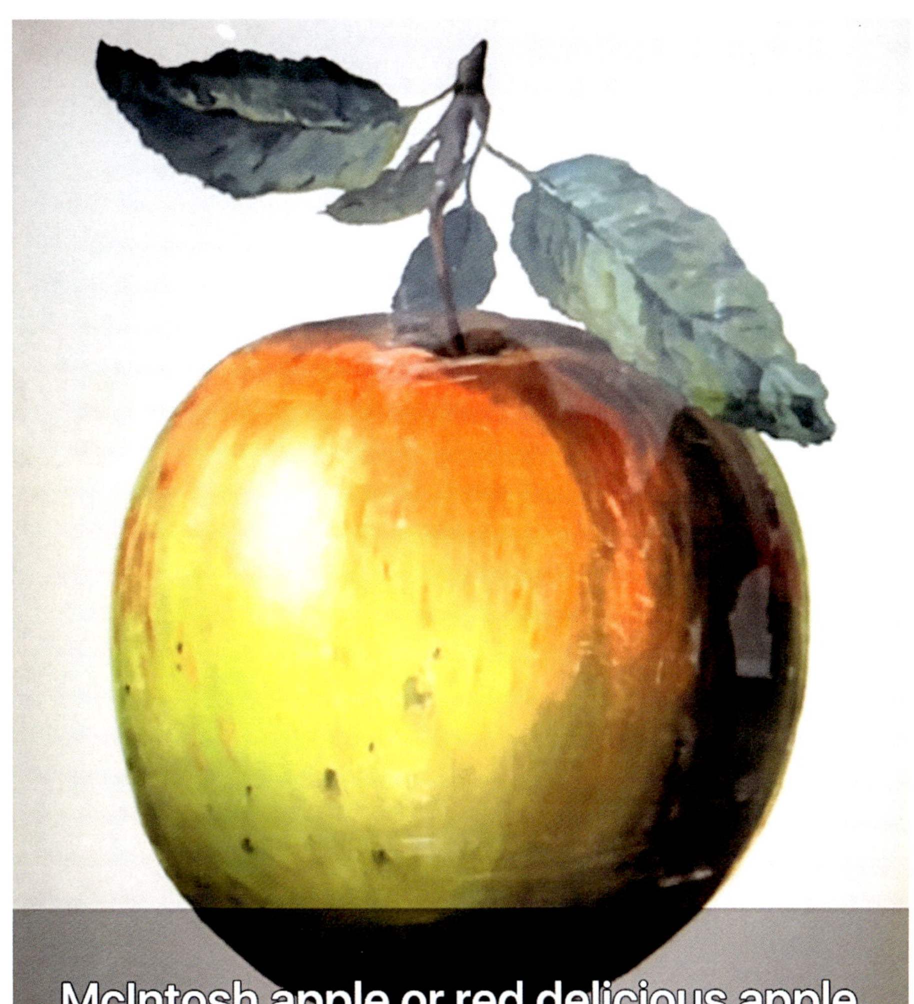

McIntosh apple or red delicious apple

Incident Title:*The Interview*
Date Incident Was Transferred To The Public: **March 20/17**
Environment In Which Incident Took Place: **My Cité studio; part of the *Honeymoon In Paradise***

Category: **Performance**
Type Of Incident (Ex: Displacement, Collage, Analogy): **Personification**
Media Affected/Effected (Ex: Canvas, Body, Objects): **Language, text**
Primary Impulse/Inspiration/Cause Of Incident (Ex: Encounter, Experience, Conversation): **Conversation**

Name Of Person First Notified: **Daniela Dill**
Was A Relative Notified? **No**

Description of the event, including any obvious incident-related circumstances:

Being outside of my usual surroundings made me reflect on my art making process. I tried to separate myself from my art practice as if we were two entities, asking her-him-it questions about our relationship and how we want to work together. Throughout our conversation we touched on ethics, politics and play. You can see in a transcript of one of our dialogues, that my practice claims to be more clever than I, when I re-read it, it became clear that we were ethically different.

The Interview was shown as an ongoing rehearsal in which the text was embodied by an actress who took the role of both: the artist (me) and the practice (mine). Throughout the rehearsal the actress repeated passages in different positions and with different tones which created and revealed new layers of meaning.

Supportive Measures Taken Prior To Incident

[Check All That Apply]:
- ☒ Increased level of observation
- ☒ Vivid cultural environment
- ☒ Artist integrated into the local art scene
- ☐ Professional group discussions

Motivation (mark appropriate):
enthusiasm obsession pleasure pain insomnia struggle deadline Other:

Cognitive Factors

[Check All That Apply]:
- ☒ Perception, attention
- ☐ Wondering
- ☐ Imagination, creativity
- ☐ Experimentation, play
- ☐ Planning, orientation
- ☒ Learning
- ☒ Memory
- ☒ Argumentation
- ☒ Introspection
- ☐ Extroversion
- ☐ Other:

Environment[s] In Which The Incident Was Conceived And/Or Executed

[Answer with Yes or No]:
Studio **Yes**
Library **No**
Hardware store **No**
Workshops **No**
Space with adequate lighting **Yes**
Possibility for accommodation **Yes**

Acoustic environment (mark appropriate):
Music Noise Silence Other:
Cleanliness of environment (mark appropriate):
Clean Cluttered area Messy Other:
Recreational activities (mark appropriate):
Dancing Swimming Running Other:
Wifi (mark appropriate):
No connection Poor connection Good connection
Other: **Café next to the Seine, Paris**

Support

Name[s] And Function[s] Of The Person[s] Involved:
Daniela Dill, performer
Tomke Braun, editing advisor
Photos by Akira Takaishi

Assistant's Advice was useful?
Needed More Advice That Was Not Available?
Advice Safely Used By Affected Artist[s]?
Other:

Functional Factors

[Check All That Apply]:
- ☒ Desire
- ☒ Loneliness
- ☐ Connectedness
- ☒ Electricity
- ☐ Food
- ☒ Drinks
- ☒ Emotional balance
- ☐ Emotional unbalance
- ☐ Other:

Mobility

Position[s] taken (mark appropriate):
sitting standing lying moving rolling

Body part[s] involved (mark appropriate):
hands fingers arms eyes
ears head legs mouth toes
heart lungs hips Other:

Equipment Used To Manifest The Incident

[Check All That Apply]:
- ☒ Computer
- ☒ Chair
- ☐ Hot plate
- ☐ Camera
- ☐ Smartphone
- ☐ Projector
- ☐ Bicycle
- ☒ Bed
- ☐ Other:

Material Evidence With This Report

Mark Applicable Description[s] Of Accompanying Material:

1st Page: Documentation Installation view
Video Still Reproduction Other:

2nd Page: Documentation Installation view
Video Still Reproduction Other:

3rd Page: Documentation Installation view
Video Still Reproduction Other:
The Interview (excerpt)

4th Page: Documentation Installation view
Video Still Reproduction Other:

5th Page: Documentation Installation view
Video Still Reproduction Other:

Completed by Gabriel Hensche   **Signature:**

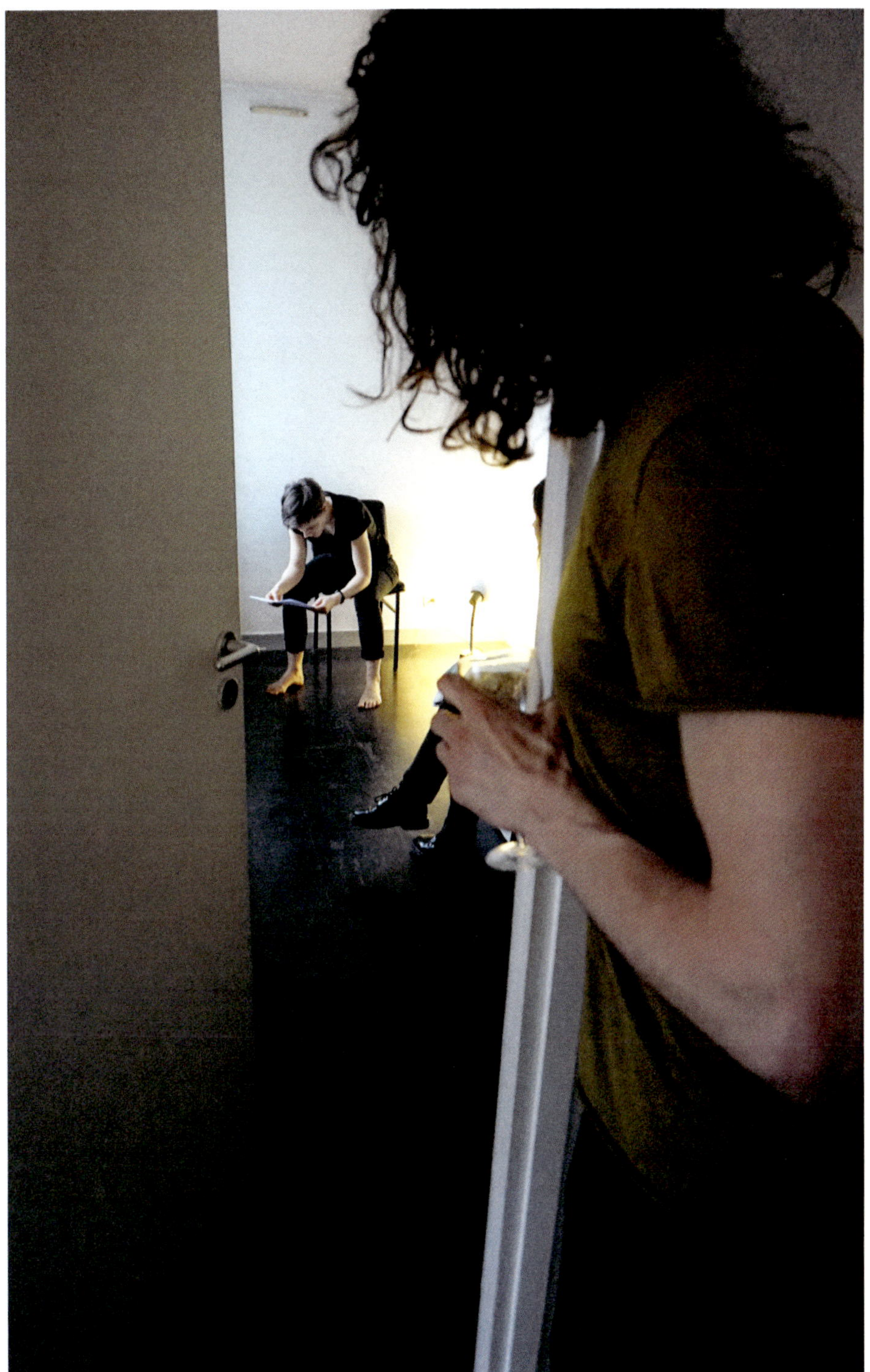

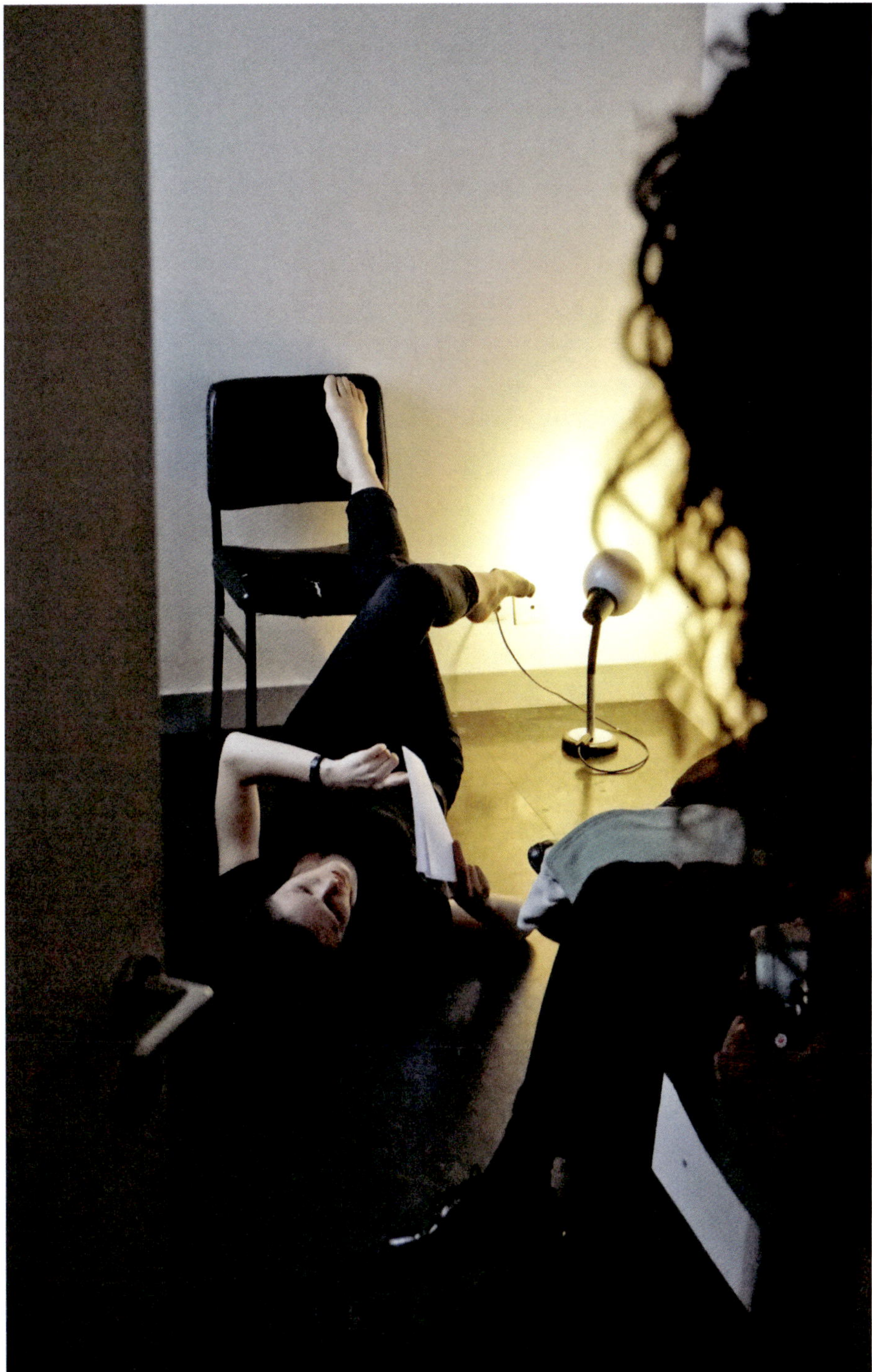

[...]

Practice: Every project not only has to change its shape in conversation with people, but it also should enter a dialogue with the situation and the circumstances it emerges from and of course, the artist is a crucial part of that process.

Artist: That means, in the end, you potentially capitalise on my whole personal life?

P: Well...

A: That's horrible.

P: Come one, I know that you enjoy it.

A: No.

P: Yes, you do.

A: Ok, you seem to be more clever than me.

P: I am.

[...]

Incident Title: *Honeymoon In Paradise*
Date Incident Was Transferred To The Public: **March 20/17**
Environment In Which Incident Took Place: **My Cité studio**

Category: **Social space**
Type Of Incident (Ex: Displacement, Collage, Analogy): **Constructed situation**
Media Affected/Effected (Ex: Canvas, Body, Objects): **Various artistic practices**
Primary Impulse/Inspiration/Cause Of Incident (Ex: Encounter, Experience, Conversation): **Conversation**

Name Of Person First Notified: **Ashlee Conery**
Was A Relative Notified? **No**

Description of the event, including any obvious incident-related circumstances:

Thinking about La Cité Internationale des Arts residency as a kind of honeymoon for artists and their practice's—a time of focused attention away from the distractions and routines of one's actual life—curator FormContent and I, invited the other artists-in-residence to introduce their respective practices over dinner. Connections and dialogues were formed over wine between practice and practice, artist and artist, practice and artist, and artist and practice. These comprised not only of language but images, readings, stretches, rehearsals, print training, notebooking, dj-ing, hummus and dancing.

Artists/curators implicated in incident: Aziyadé Baudouin-Talec, Daniela Dill, Simone Etter, FormContent, Rotem Gerstel, Anita Holtsclaw, Laura Hunt, France Manoush Sahatdjian, Christoph Poetsch, Eden Sarna, Akira Takaishi, Julia Wirsching

Supportive Measures Taken Prior To Incident

[Check All That Apply]:
- ☒ Increased level of observation
- ☒ Vivid cultural environment
- ☒ Artist integrated into the local art scene
- ☒ Professional group discussions

Motivation (mark appropriate):
enthusiasm | obsession | pleasure | pain insomnia struggle deadline Other:

Cognitive Factors

[Check All That Apply]:
- ☒ Perception, attention
- ☒ Wondering
- ☐ Imagination, creativity
- ☒ Experimentation, play
- ☒ Planning, orientation
- ☒ Learning
- ☐ Memory
- ☐ Argumentation
- ☐ Introspection
- ☒ Extroversion
- ☐ Other:

Environment(s) In Which The Incident Was Conceived And/Or Executed

[Answer with Yes or No]:
Studio **Yes**
Library **No**
Hardware store **No**
Workshops **No**
Space with adequate lighting **Yes**
Possibility for accommodation **Yes**

Acoustic environment (mark appropriate):
Music Noise Silence Other:

Cleanliness of environment (mark appropriate):
Clean | Cluttered area Messy Other:

Recreational activities (mark appropriate):
Dancing | Swimming Running Other:

Wifi (mark appropriate):
No connection Poor connection Good connection
Other:

Support

Name(s) And Function(s) Of The Person(s) Involved:
FormContent, co-host

Assistant's Advice was useful? **Yes**
Needed More Advice That Was Not Available? **No**
Advice Safely Used By Affected Artist(s)? **Yes**
Other:

Functional Factors

[Check All That Apply]:
- ☒ Desire
- ☐ Loneliness
- ☒ Connectedness
- ☒ Electricity
- ☒ Food
- ☒ Drinks
- ☒ Emotional balance
- ☐ Emotional unbalance
- ☐ Other:

Mobility

Position(s) taken (mark appropriate):
sitting | standing | lying | moving | rolling

Body part(s) involved (mark appropriate):
hands | fingers | arms eyes |
ears | head legs mouth | toes
heart lungs hips | Other:

Equipment Used To Manifest The Incident

[Check All That Apply]:
- ☒ Computer
- ☒ Chair
- ☒ Hot plate
- ☐ Camera
- ☒ Smartphone
- ☒ Projector
- ☐ Bicycle
- ☒ Bed
- ☒ Other:
Extra chairs and drinking glasses

Material Evidence With This Report

Mark Applicable Description(s) Of Accompanying Material:

1st Page: Documentation | Installation view Video Still Reproduction Other:

2nd Page: Documentation Installation view Video Still Reproduction Other:
Invitation letter

3rd Page: Documentation | Installation view Video Still Reproduction Other:

4th Page: Documentation Installation view Video Still Reproduction Other:

5th Page: Documentation Installation view Video Still Reproduction Other:

Completed by Gabriel Hensche　　　　Signature:

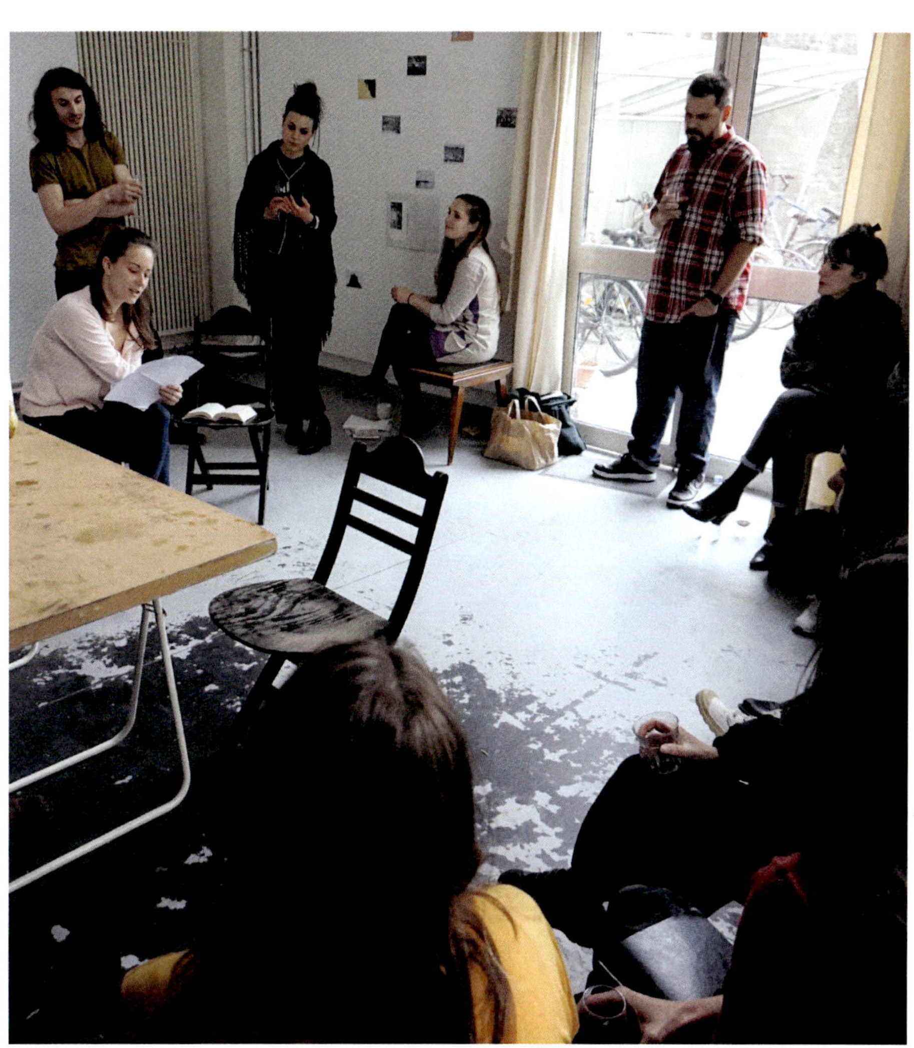

Dear Guest,

I thought of this residency as a kind of honeymoon, where my art practice and I could spend a lot of quality time together. But after a while our relationship began to feel a bit monotonous and so we decided to organize a few gatherings—Closed Studios—in order to meet other artists and practices. My practice has found support in these introductions, while I have remained slightly isolated. While not necessarily wanting the familiarity which may subjugate my subjecthood to traditional group dynamics, the intimacy my practice has found in these dinners is something I know will benefit our relationship in the long run.

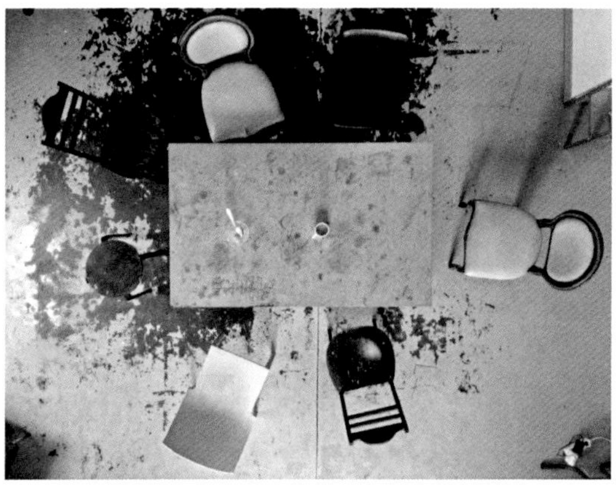

FormContent came to visit us in Paris and we decided to host the next Closed Studio together. But as you know within our studios there are not enough chairs, glasses or spoons for a gathering over two or three. Discussing this with FormContent brought forth the realisation that what our relationship has been missing is the bits of home which bring comfort to one's daily routine. Certainly we have developed a new routine as I am sure you have to, I lean on my practice as she/he/it leans on me, but the life we left behind continues on with news of its events reaching us every so often. We have gone back in the midst of being here, however that only seemed to leave us more alienated in both places. The residency and economic realities have made it difficult, for you as well I'm sure, to bring in family, friends, lovers and works from outside. I have heard rumours, however, that some of these things have been snuck into the complex and wondered if anyone might consider sharing them on this occasion?

As we are all coupled here, in accordance with the residency—
though on occasion I have heard residents have been aban-
doned by their practices mid-residency—this is an invitation for
you and your practice. If your practice for whatever reason
cannot come please bring something you have made together.

As well, if you should have any of the following we ask you to
bring them too:

- a chair
- a glass
- a spoon
- a friend
- a family member

Please let us know via e-mail if you're both able to attend (RSVP
is required) for this Closed Studio and which things you can
bring. It will be held at our studio in Cité Internationale des Arts,
No. 2051 (Marais, in front of the Café des Arts), on Monday,
March 20th, 5 pm.

FormContent will begin with introductions followed by dinner
and an open discussion on routines, happenings and
voids between you and yours in the context of the residency.

We are looking forward to hearing from you.

Best,
Gabriel & FormContent

P.S. for your practice we can offer: a projector, a speaker, a wall,
a table, space and time (15 min).

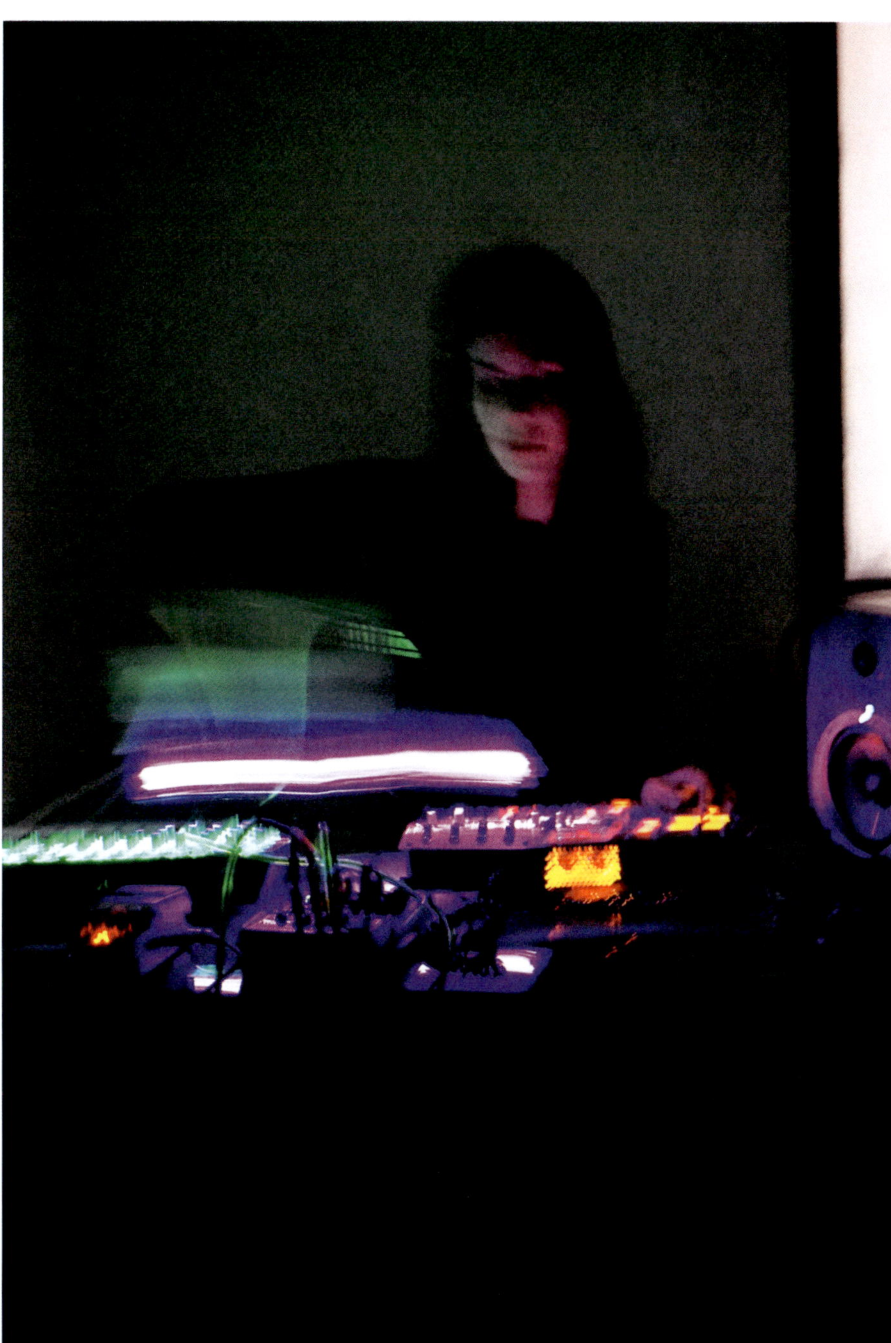

Incident Title:*Last One Out Turn Off The Lights*
Date Incident Was Transferred To The Public: **June 18—July 7/17**
Environment In Which Incident Took Place: **Galerie l'inlassable, Paris**

Category: **Curatorial project**
Type Of Incident (Ex: Displacement, Collage, Analogy): **Collective effort**
Media Affected/Effected (Ex: Canvas, Body, Objects): **Various artistic practices**
Primary Impulse/Inspiration/Cause Of Incident (Ex: Encounter, Experience, Conversation): **Experience**

Name Of Person First Notified: **Sarah Mercadante**
Was A Relative Notified?**Yes**

Description of the event, including any obvious incident-related circumstances:

Based on the question, 'how do residencies influence artists and their art practice?' I initiated an exhibition entitled *Last One Out Turn Off The Lights.* Twenty artists, that I met during my residency, were asked to fit their art practice into a galleries vitrine. There were two simple rules: each artist had 24 hours, from midnight to midnight, to prepare, install and perform a work in the window, that represented, re-enacted and reflected on their art making process. I found this task allowed the artists to show a new side of their practice.

Beyond the vitrine, the main gallery space was used as a 'future archive' which stored all the materials that would be used by the artists. Labels indicated to whom they belonged and the date of their performance. Whereas usually exhibitions show what was made in the past, here we presented the materials that would become a work in the future. After the opening each day, one artist would take their contents from the gallery space and use them for their 24h performance in the vitrine. The whole artistic process, from production to de-installation was on view for the public.

Artists/curators implicated in incident: Stéphanie Baechler, Sascha Brosamer, Sophie Dupont, Simone Etter, Rotem Gerstel, Sarah Haddou, Gabriel Hensche, Anita Holtsclaw, Sophie Innmann, Claudia Kübler, Sarah Mercadante, Petra Mrša, Abi Tariq/Honi Ryan, France Manoush Sahatdjian, Eden Sarna, Goran Škofić, Laëtitia Striffling, Akira Takaishi, Riki Werdenigg, Julia Wirsching

Supportive Measures Taken Prior To Incident
[Check All That Apply]:
☒ Increased level of observation
☒ Vivid cultural environment
☒ Artist integrated into the local art scene
☒ Professional group discussions
Motivation (mark appropriate):
  |enthusiasm| obsession pleasure pain insomnia
  struggle deadline Other:

Cognitive Factors
[Check All That Apply]:
☒ Perception, attention
☐ Wondering
☐ Imagination, creativity
☐ Experimentation, play
☒ Planning, orientation
☒ Learning
☐ Memory
☒ Argumentation
☐ Introspection
☒ Extroversion
☐ Other:

Environment(s) In Which The Incident
Was Conceived And/Or Executed
[Answer with Yes or No]:
Studio **Yes**
Library **Yes**
Hardware store **Yes**
Workshops **No**
Space with adequate lighting **Yes**
Possibility for accommodation **Yes**

Acoustic environment (mark appropriate):
  Music |Noise| Silence Other:
Cleanliness of environment (mark appropriate):
  Clean |Cluttered area| Messy Other:
Recreational activities (mark appropriate):
  |Dancing| Swimming Running Other:
Wifi (mark appropriate):
  No connection Poor connection Good connection
  |Other:| **Gallery/Gallery's vitrine**

Support
Name(s) And Function(s) Of The Person(s) Involved:
Sarah Mercadante, co-curator
John Ferrère, Ulysse Geissler, gallerists
Juana Valentina Monroy, assistant

Assistant's Advice was useful? **Yes/No**
Needed More Advice That Was Not Available? **Yes/No**
Advice Safely Used By Affected Artist(s)? **Yes/No**
  Other: **This incident was shaped by all participating artists**

Functional Factors
[Check All That Apply]:
☒ Desire
☐ Loneliness
☒ Connectedness
☒ Electricity
☒ Food
☒ Drinks
☒ Emotional balance
☒ Emotional unbalance
☐ Other:

Mobility
Position(s) taken (mark appropriate):
  |sitting| |standing| lying |moving| rolling

Body part(s) involved (mark appropriate):
  |hands| |fingers| |arms| |eyes|
  |ears| |head| |legs| |mouth| |toes|
  |heart| |lungs| |hips| Other:

Equipment Used To Manifest The Incident
[Check All That Apply]:
☒ Computer
☒ Chair
☐ Hot plate
☒ Camera
☒ Smartphone
☐ Projector
☒ Bicycle
☐ Bed
☒ Other:
White paint, key for the gallery's vitrine

Material Evidence With This Report
Mark Applicable Description(s) Of Accompanying Material:

1st Page: Documentation |Installation view|
           Video Still Reproduction Other:
Applies to all pages of the incident
2nd Page: Documentation Installation view
           Video Still Reproduction Other:

3rd Page: Documentation Installation view
           Video Still Reproduction Other:

4th Page: Documentation Installation view
           Video Still Reproduction Other:

5th Page: Documentation Installation view
           Video Still Reproduction Other:

Completed by Gabriel Hensche

Signature: 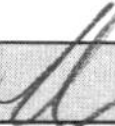

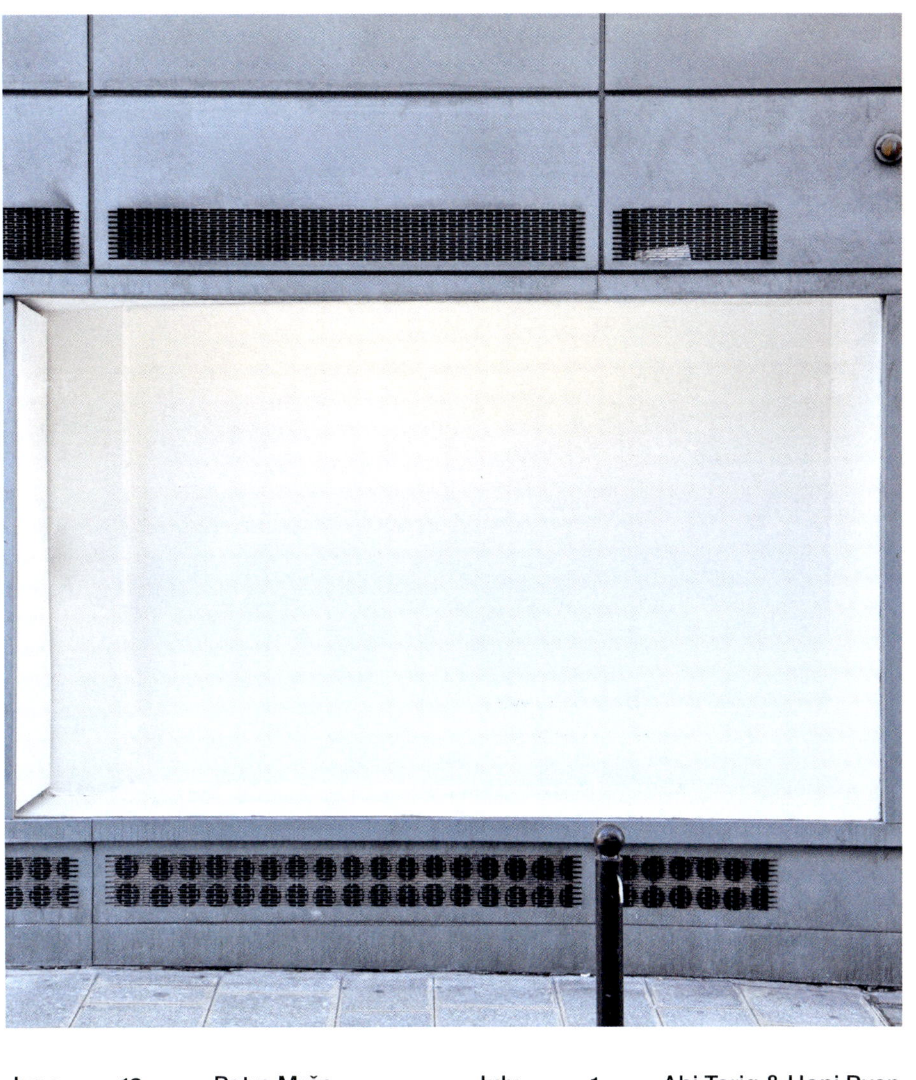

June	19	Petra Mrša	July	1	Abi Tariq & Honi Ryan
	20	Sophie Dupont		2	Sarah Haddou
	21	Riki Werdenigg		3	France Manoush
	22	Claudia Kübler			Sahatdjian
	23	Eden Sarna		4	Goran Škofić
	24	Sascha Brosamer		5	Simone Etter
	25	Rotem Gerstel		6	Anita Holtsclaw
	26	Gabriel Hensche		7	Sophie Innmann
	27	Laëtitia Striffling			
	28	Stéphanie Baechler			
	29	Akira Takaishi			
	30	Julia Wirsching			

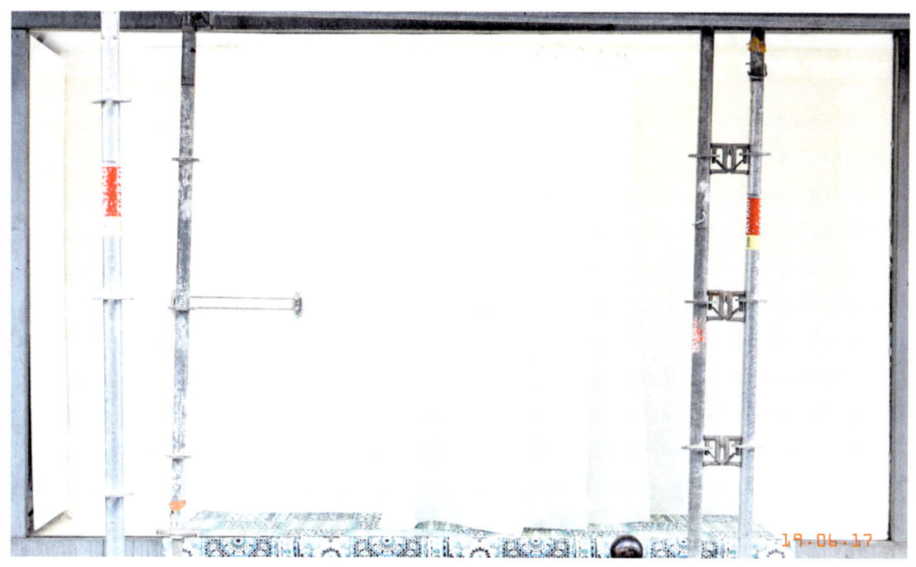
19.06.17

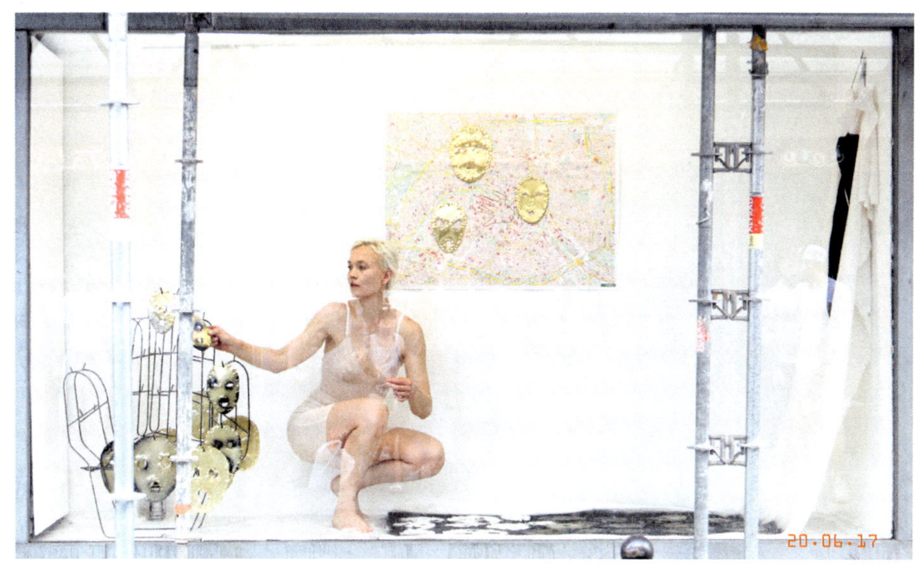

20.06.17

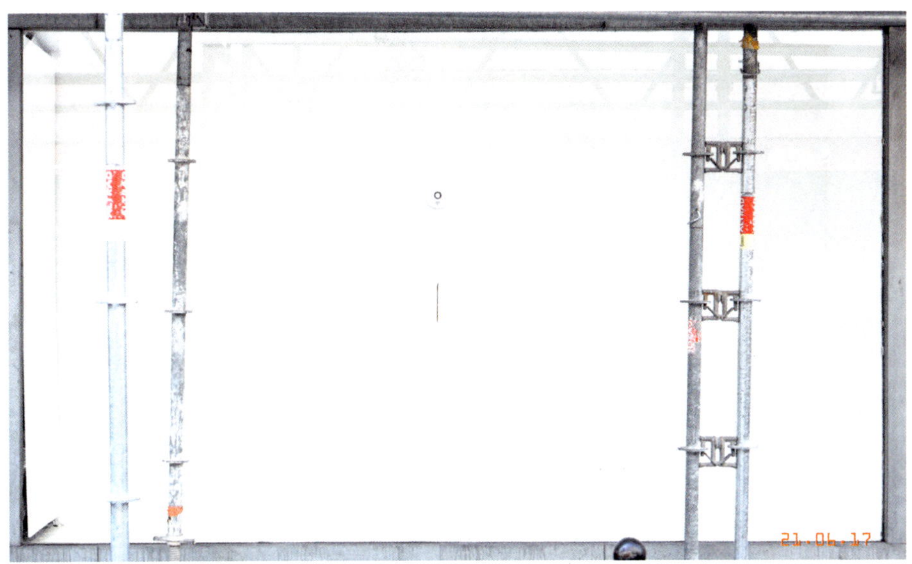

21.06.17

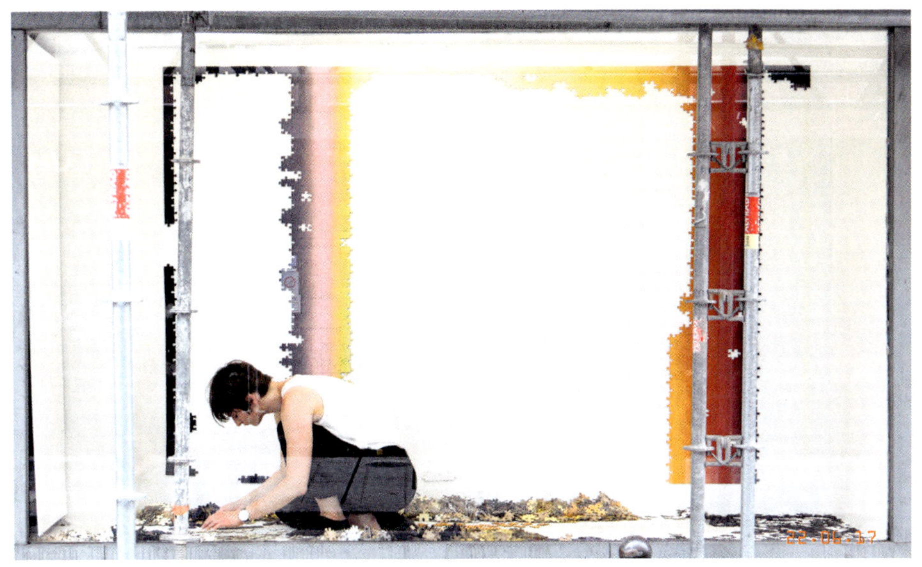

22·06·17

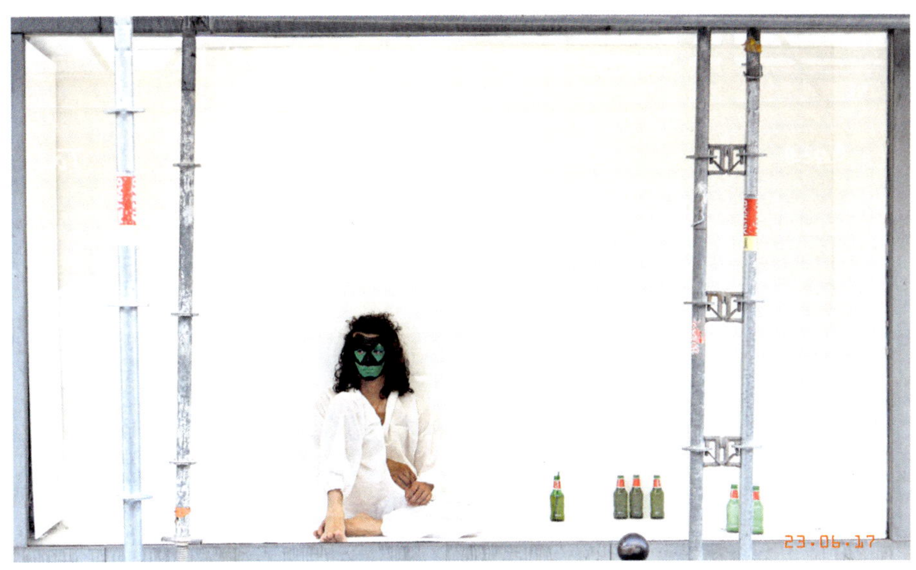
23.06.17

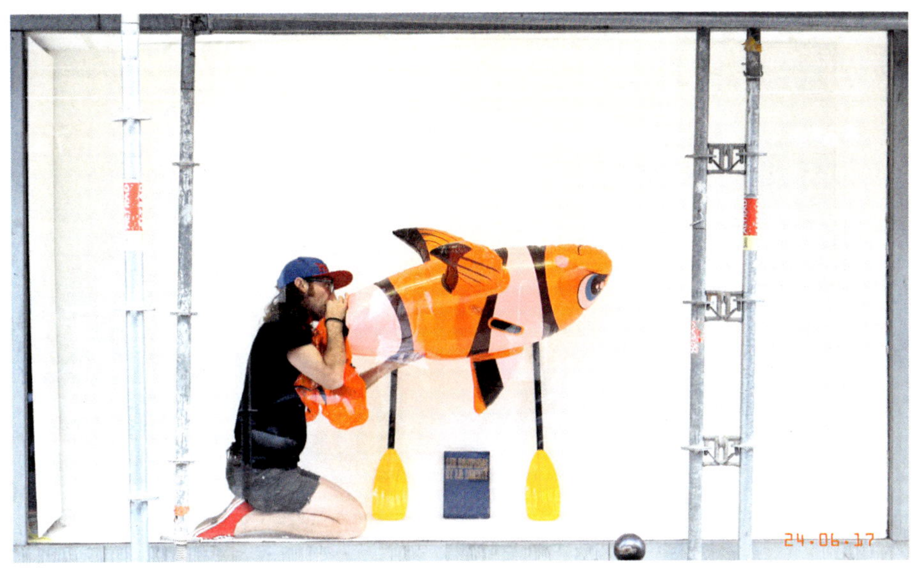
24·06·17

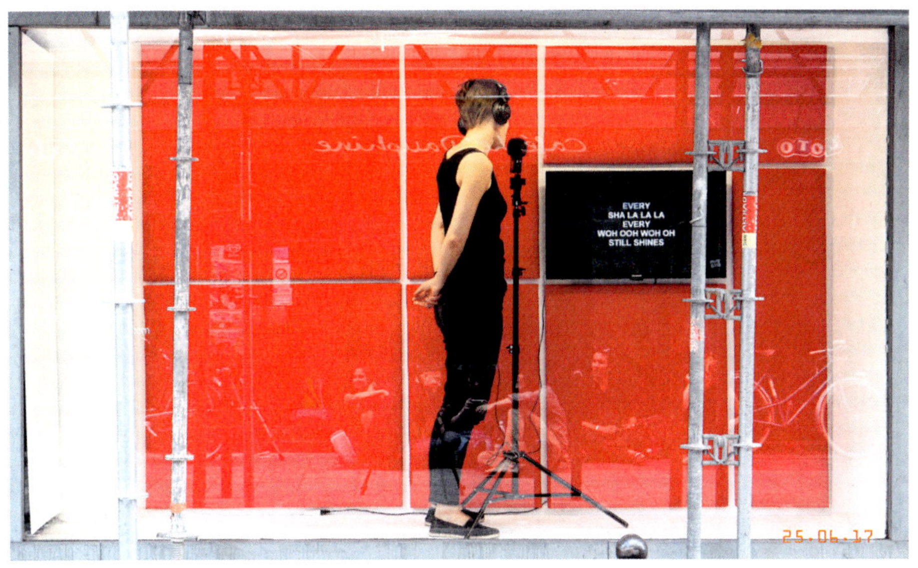
EVERY
SHA LA LA LA
EVERY
WOH OOH WOH OH
STILL SHINES

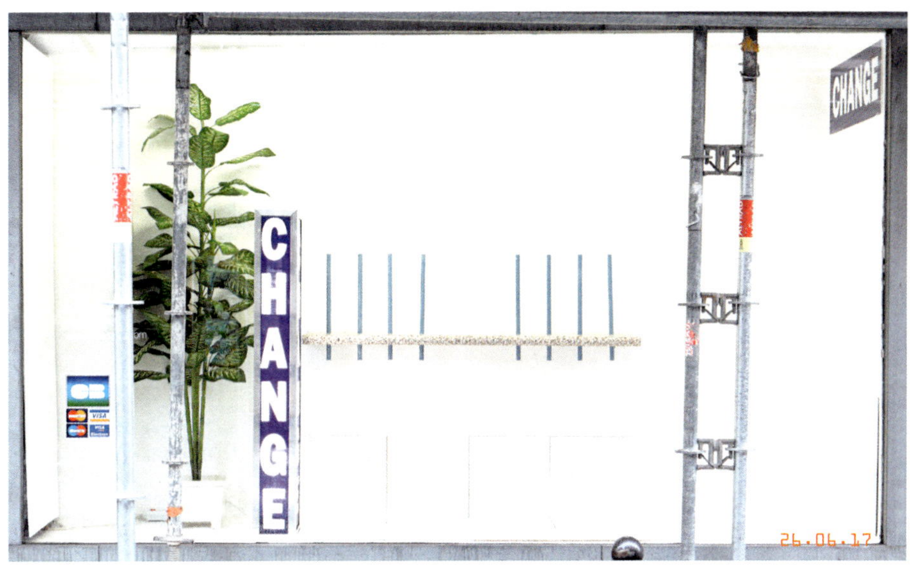
CHANGE
CHANGE
26.06.17

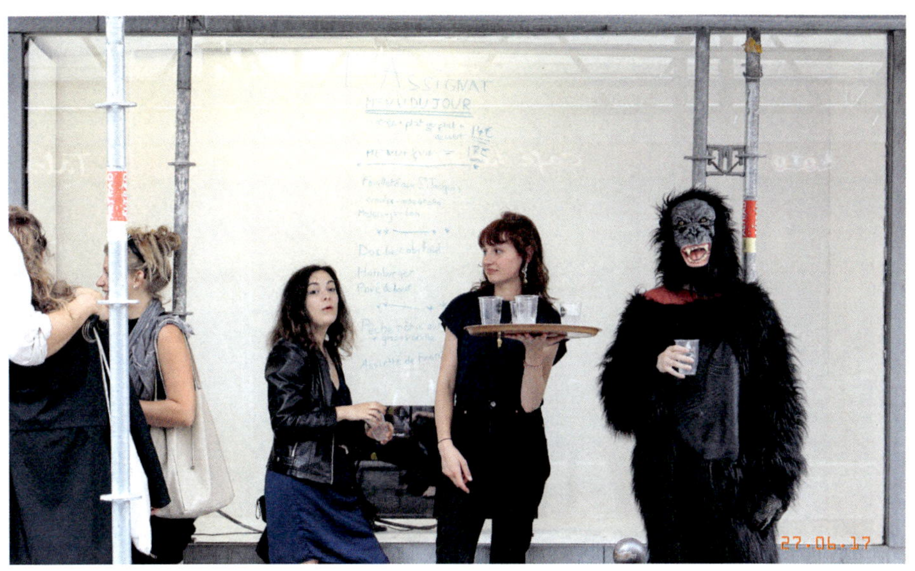

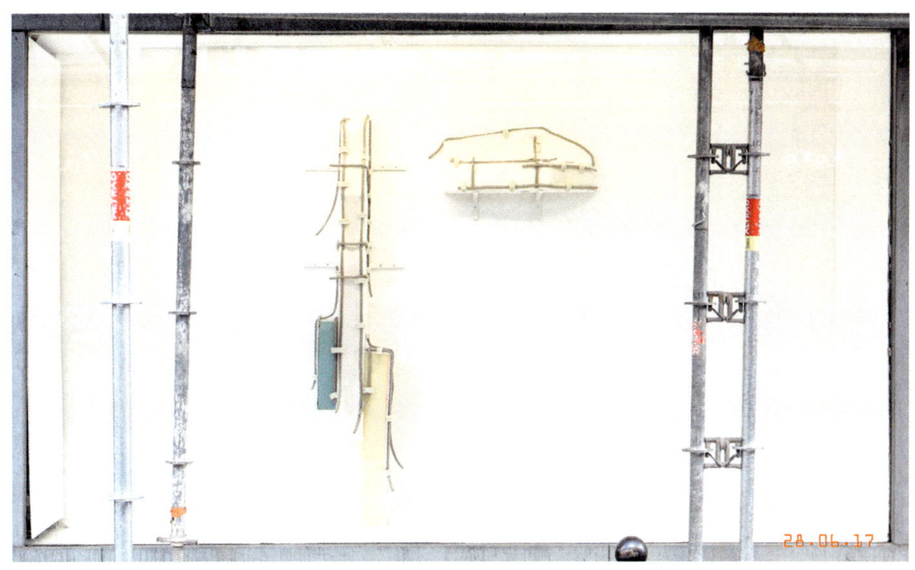
28.06.17

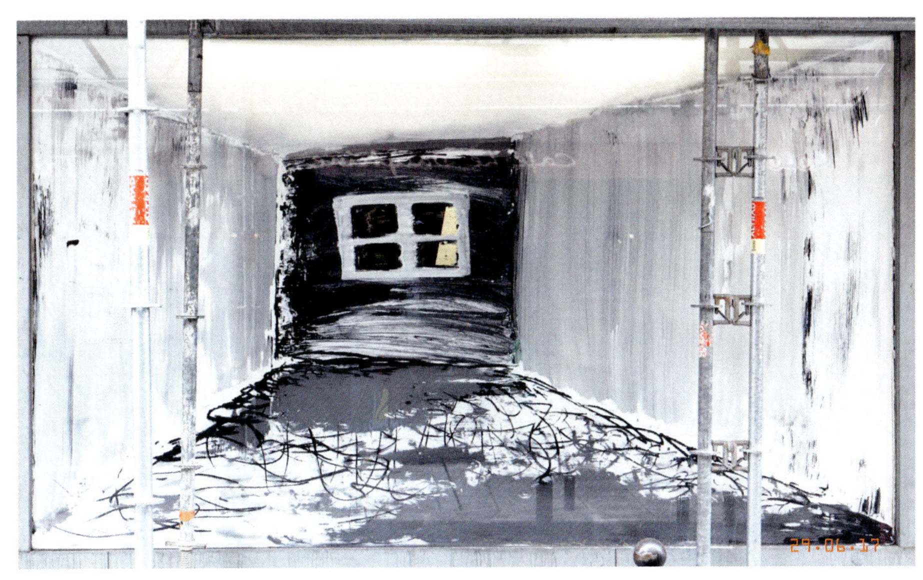

29·06·17

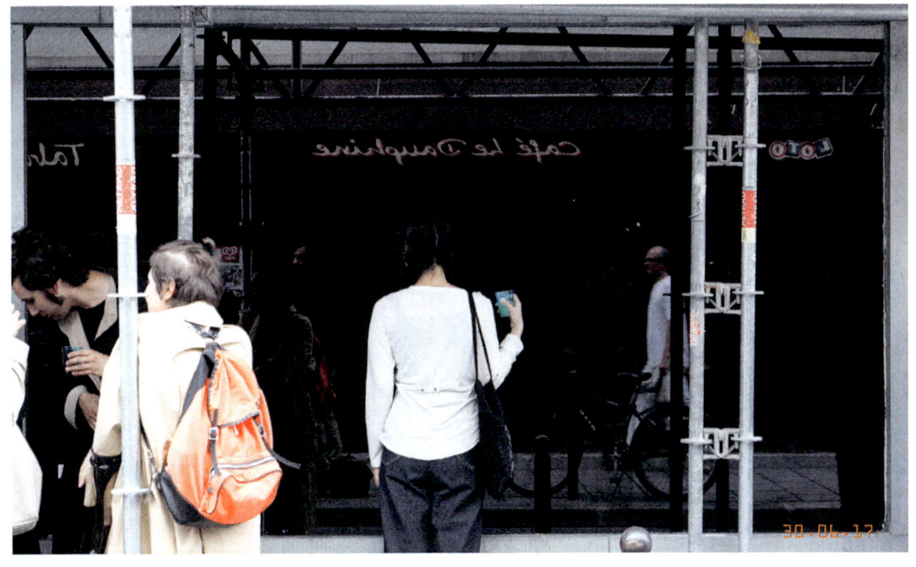

Café Le Dauphine
LOTO
30·06·17

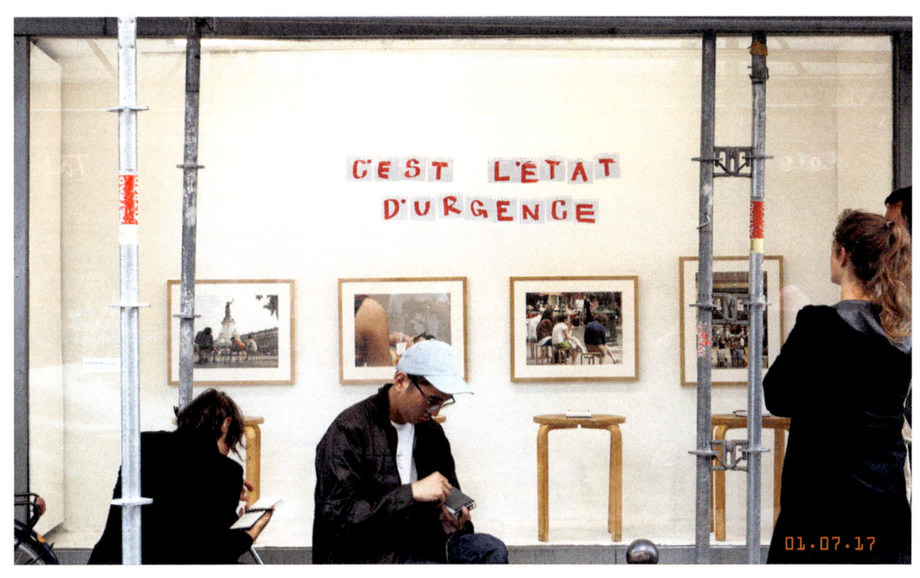

C'EST L'ETAT
D'URGENCE
01.07.17

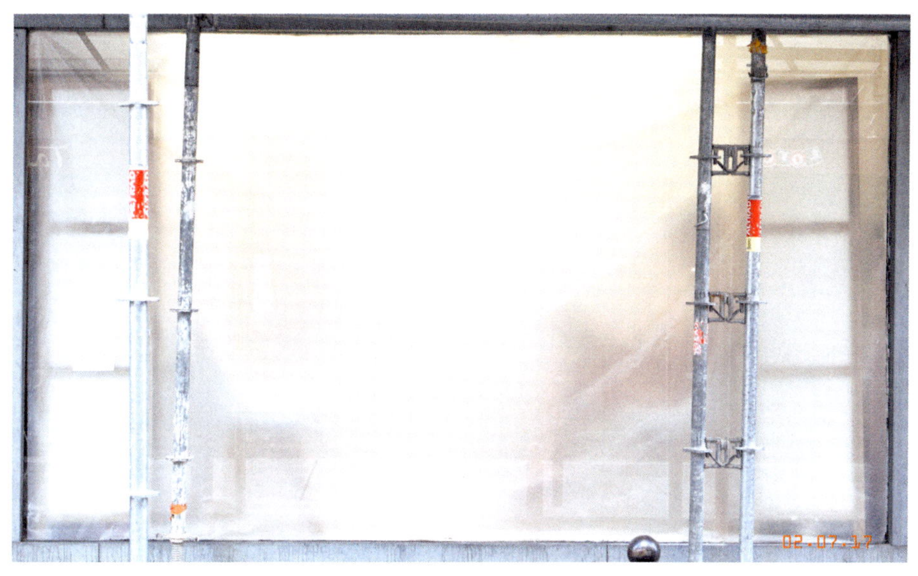

02-07-17

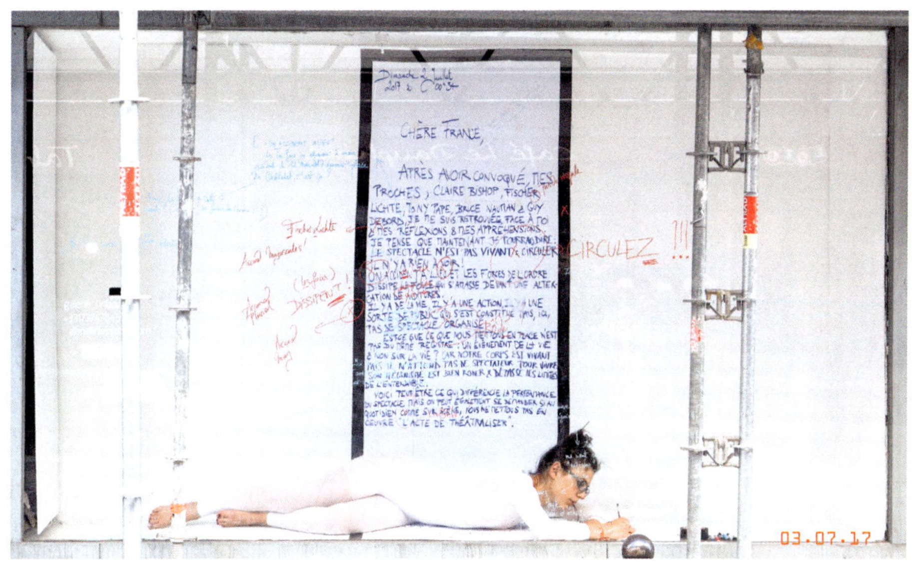

Dimanche 2 Juillet
2017 à 00:34

CHÈRE FRANCE,

APRÈS AVOIR CONVOQUÉ, MES PROCHES, CLAIRE BISHOP, FISCHER LICHTE, TONY PAPE, BRUCE NAUMAN & GUY DEBORD, JE ME SUIS RETROUVÉE FACE À TOI & MES RÉFLEXIONS & MES APPRÉHENSIONS. JE PENSE QUE MAINTENANT JE POURRAI DIRE : LE SPECTACLE N'EST PAS VIVANT & CIRCULER, CIRCULEZ !!! ... Y'A RIEN À VOIR !
ON ACCIDENT A LIEU ET LES FORCES DE L'ORDRE DISSIPENT LA FOULE QUI S'AMASSE DEVANT UNE ALTERCATION DE VOITURES.
IL Y A DE LA VIE, IL Y A UNE ACTION, IL Y A UNE SORTE DE PUBLIC QUI S'EST CONSTITUÉ MAIS, ICI, PAS DE SPECTACLE ORGANISÉ ?!
EST-CE QUE CE QUE VOUS METTONS EN PLACE N'EST PAS DU MÊME REGISTRE : UN ÉVÉNEMENT DE LA VIE & NON SUR LA VIE ? CAR NOTRE CORPS EST VIVANT MAIS IL N'ATTEND PAS LE SPECTATEUR POUR VIVRE, SON MÉCANISME EST BIEN ROVER & DE PAS LES LIMITES DE L'ENTENDABLE.
VOICI PEUT-ÊTRE CE QUI DIFFÉRENCIE LA PERFORMANCE DU SPECTACLE MAIS ON PEUT ÉGALEMENT SE DEMANDER SI AU QUOTIDIEN COMME SUR SCÈNE, NOUS NE METTONS PAS EN ŒUVRE "L'ACTE DE THÉÂTRALISER".

Fischer Lichte
Accord majuscules !
(les forces) DISSIPENT !

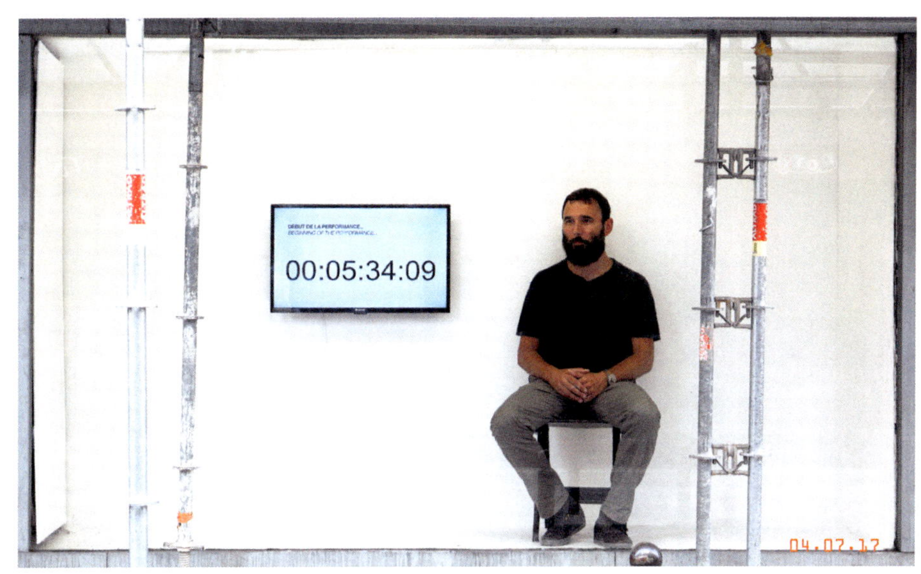

DÉBUT DE LA PERFORMANCE...
BEGINNING OF THE PERFORMANCE...
00:05:34:09

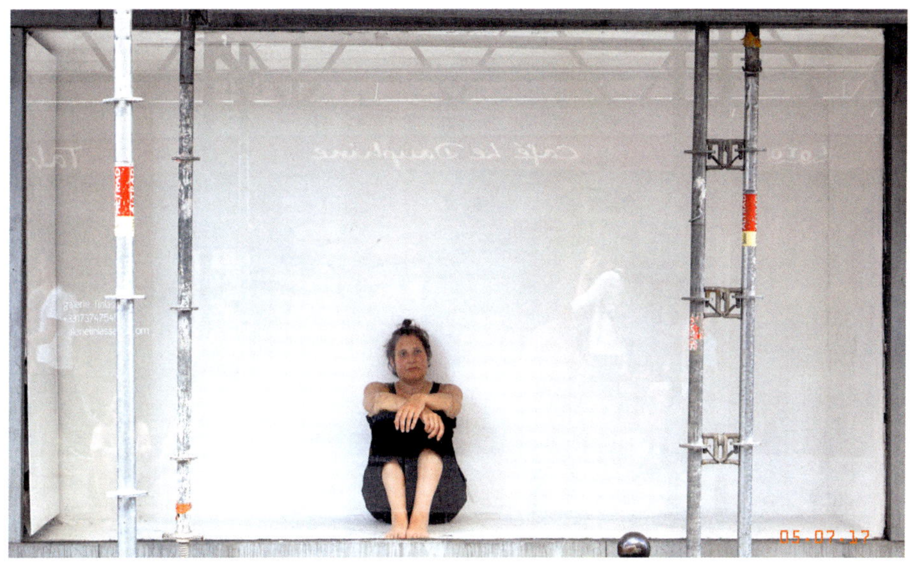

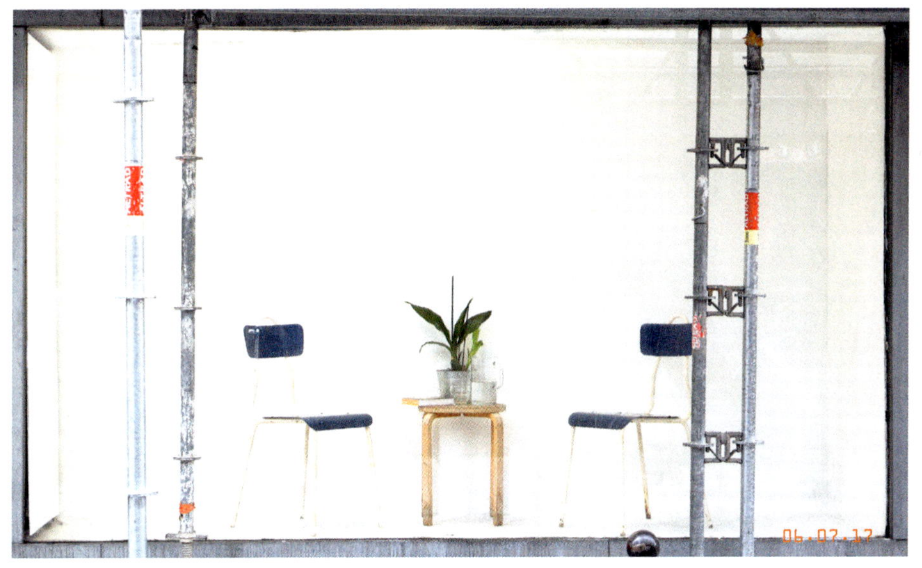
06.07.17

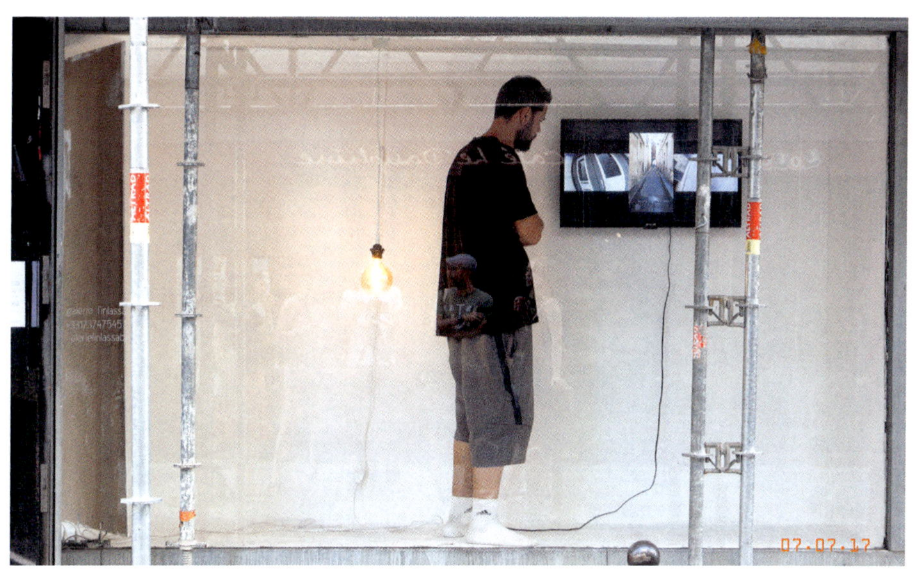

Incident Title: *Change*
Date Incident Was Transferred To The Public: **June 26/17**
Environment In Which Incident Took Place: **Galerie l'inlassable, as part of *Last One Out***

Category: **Installation**
Type Of Incident (Ex: Displacement, Collage, Analogy): **Displacement, rearrangement**
Media Affected/Effected (Ex: Canvas, Body, Objects): **Objects**
Primary Impulse/Inspiration/Cause Of Incident (Ex: Encounter, Experience, Conversation): **Encounter**

Name Of Person First Notified: **John Ferrère**
Was A Relative Notified? **Yes**

Description of the event, including any obvious incident-related circumstances:

While walking down the street on which galerie l'inlassable is located,
I noticed a money exchange shop that had all the ingredients for
a contemporary art installation; I wondered how much an alchemist
and an artist have in common? I decided to rebuild and rearrange
parts of the money exchange shop—a lightbox with the letters
C-H-A-N-G-E, pink tiles with a marble pattern, a mirror, a door handle,
a welcome desk with parts of a security grid, a fake plant and a
visa card sticker—in the gallery's vitrine that was located 20 meters
further down the road. The money exchange shop and my installation
in the gallery's window created a déjà vu like experience for pas-
sers-by; many of whom went to admire the money exchange shop
afterwards.

<table>
<tr><td colspan="2">SECTION B: Incident Report</td></tr>
<tr><td>

Supportive Measures Taken Prior To Incident
[Check All That Apply]:
- ☒ Increased level of observation
- ☒ Vivid cultural environment
- ☒ Artist integrated into the local art scene
- ☒ Professional group discussions

Motivation (mark appropriate):
enthusiasm obsession pleasure pain insomnia
struggle |deadline| |Other:| Déjà-vu

</td><td>

Functional Factors
[Check All That Apply]:
- ☒ Desire
- ☐ Loneliness
- ☐ Connectedness
- ☒ Electricity
- ☒ Food
- ☒ Drinks
- ☒ Emotional balance
- ☒ Emotional unbalance
- ☒ Other: **www.leboncoin.fr**

</td></tr>
<tr><td>

Cognitive Factors
[Check All That Apply]:
- ☒ Perception, attention
- ☒ Wondering
- ☒ Imagination, creativity
- ☒ Experimentation, play
- ☐ Planning, orientation
- ☐ Learning
- ☐ Memory
- ☐ Argumentation
- ☐ Introspection
- ☐ Extroversion
- ☐ Other:

</td><td>

Mobility
Position(s) taken (mark appropriate):
sitting standing lying |moving| rolling

Body part(s) involved (mark appropriate):
|hands| fingers arms |eyes|
ears head legs mouth toes
heart lungs hips Other:

</td></tr>
<tr><td>

Environment(s) In Which The Incident
Was Conceived And/Or Executed
(Answer with Yes or No):
Studio **Yes**
Library **Yes**
Hardware store **Yes**
Workshops **Yes**
Space with adequate lighting **Yes**
Possibility for accommodation **Yes**

Acoustic environment (mark appropriate):
Music Noise |Silence| Other:
Cleanliness of environment (mark appropriate):
Clean |Cluttered area| |Messy| Other:
Recreational activities (mark appropriate):
|Dancing| Swimming Running Other:
Wifi (mark appropriate):
No connection Poor connection |Good connection|
Other:

</td><td>

Equipment Used To Manifest The Incident
[Check All That Apply]:
- ☒ Computer
- ☐ Chair
- ☐ Hot plate
- ☐ Camera
- ☒ Smartphone
- ☐ Projector
- ☒ Bicycle
- ☐ Bed
- ☒ Other:
Tools

</td></tr>
<tr><td>

Support
Name(s) And Function(s) Of The Person(s) Involved:
Claudia Kübler, dialogue partner
Photo (2nd page) by Petra Mrša

Assistant's Advice was useful? **Yes**
Needed More Advice That Was Not Available? **Yes**
Advice Safely Used By Affected Artist(s)? **No**
Other:

</td><td>

Material Evidence With This Report
Mark Applicable Description(s) Of Accompanying
Material:

1st Page: Documentation Installation view
Video Still Reproduction |Other:|
Exchange shop next to gallery vitrine
2nd Page: Documentation Installation view
Video Still Reproduction |Other:|
Installation view at exhibition opening
3rd Page: Documentation Installation view
Video Still Reproduction |Other:|
Installation view in the vitrine
4th Page: Documentation Installation view
Video Still Reproduction Other:

5th Page: Documentation Installation view
Video Still Reproduction Other:

</td></tr>
<tr><td>Completed by Gabriel Hensche</td><td>Signature:</td></tr>
</table>

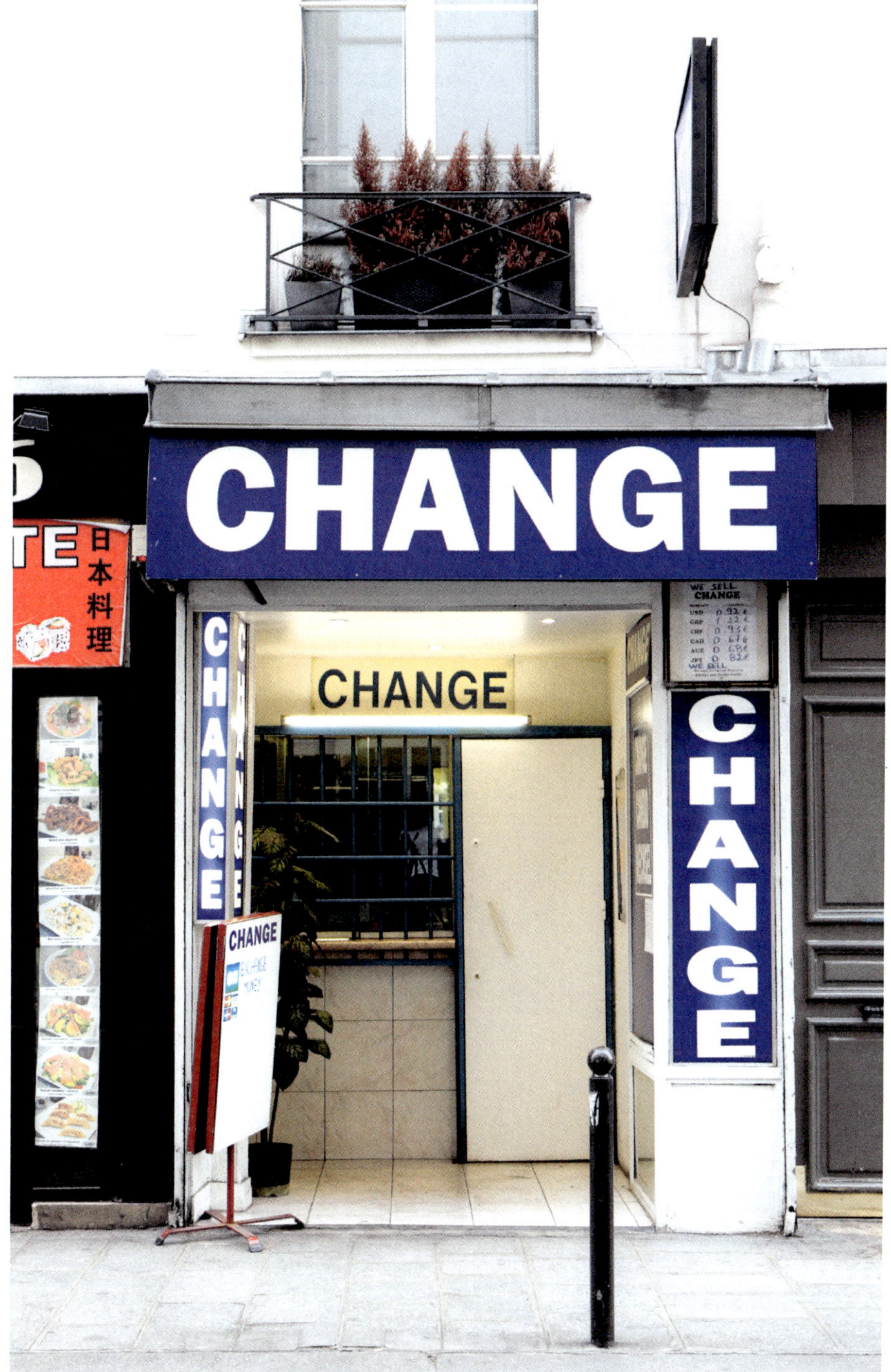
CHANGE
CHANGE
CHANGE
CHANGE
CHANGE
CHANGE
TE
日本料理
WE SELL
CHANGE
USD   0.93 €
GBP   1.22 €
CHF   0.93 €
CAD   0.67 €
AUE   0.68 €
JPY   0.82 €
WE SELL
EXCHANGE
MONEY

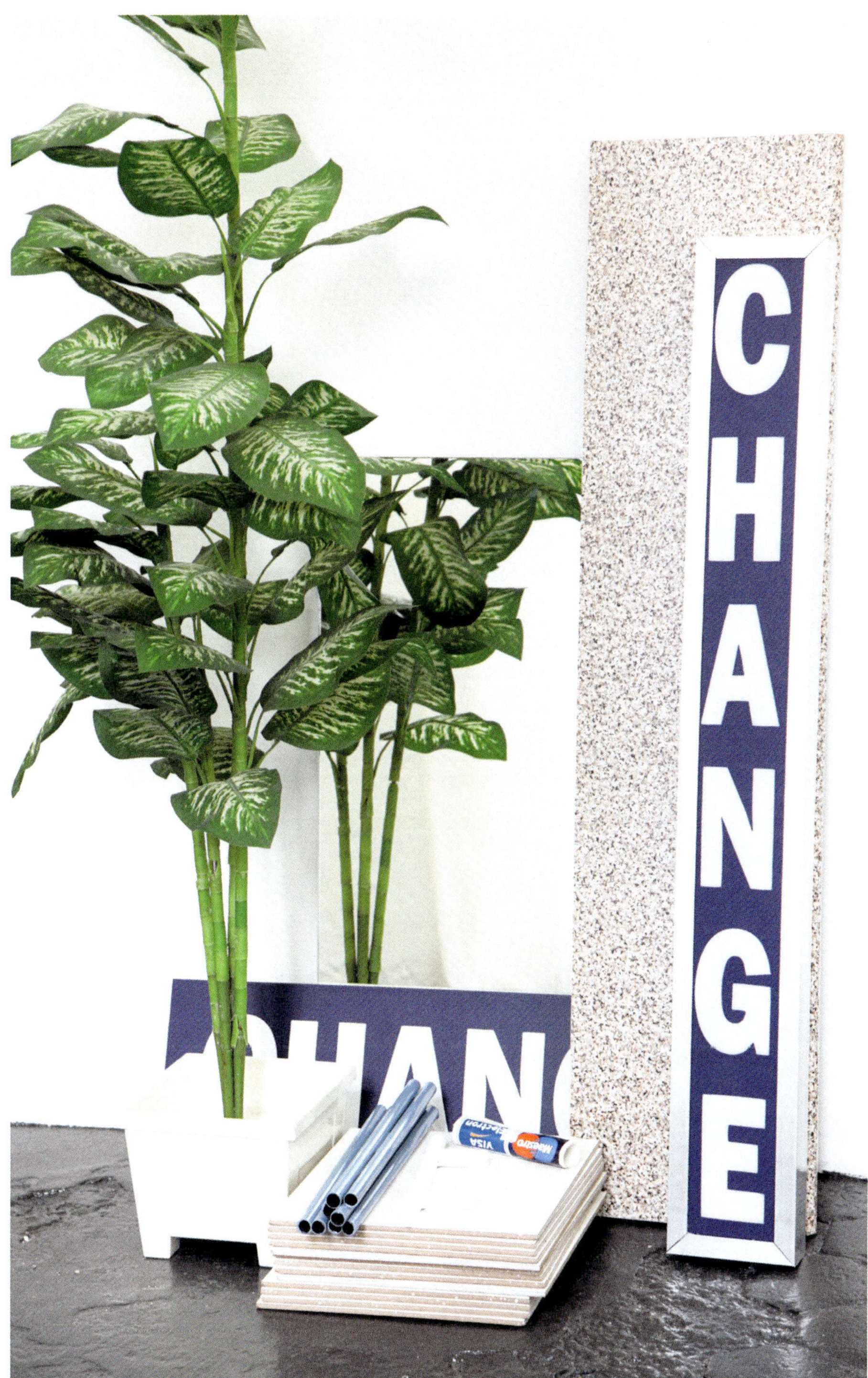

CHANGE
CHANGE
VISA
Maestro

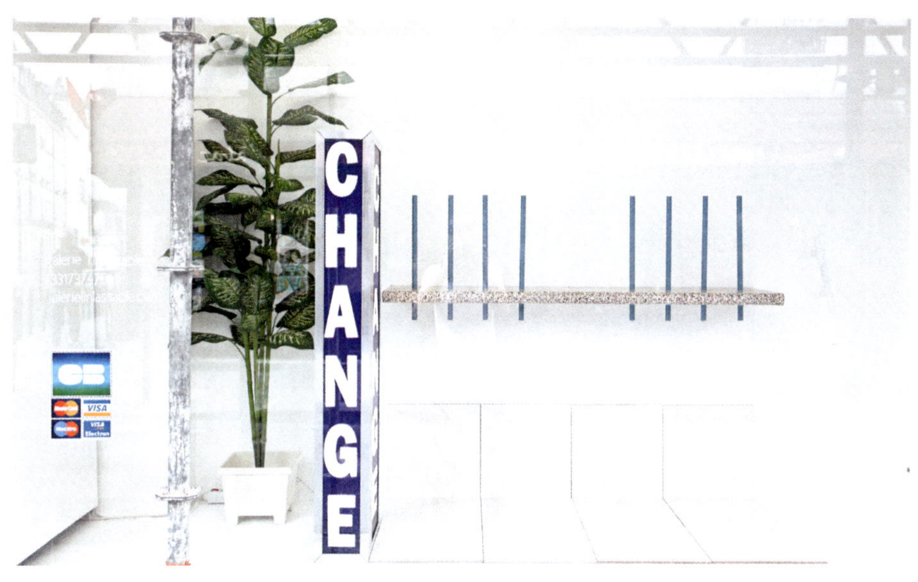

CHANGE
GB
MasterCard
VISA
Maestro
VISA
Electron

Incident Title: *The Six Month Residency*
Date Incident Was Transferred To The Public: **April 22/17**
Environment In Which Incident Took Place: **My Cité studio, part of the exhibition** *Open Yard*

Category: **Installation**
Type Of Incident (Ex: Displacement, Collage, Analogy): **Displacement, rearrangement**
Media Affected/Effected (Ex: Canvas, Body, Objects): **Objects**
Primary Impulse/Inspiration/Cause Of Incident (Ex: Encounter, Experience, Conversation): **Experience**

Name Of Person First Notified: **Petra Mrša**
Was A Relative Notified? **Yes**

Description of the event, including any obvious incident-related circumstances:

I hung all the objects I brought with me for my six-month residency
at La Cité Internationale des Arts, from the ceiling of my studio.
Each object—no matter how big or small—was hung individually
which made the installation look like an exploded view drawing in
three dimensions, that allowed the viewer to examine each object
separately: smartphone, macbook, hard disc, ebook, SD-card,
mini-projector, audio recorder, bluetooth speaker, notebook, pen,
money, passport, keys, electric toothbrush, preservatives, socks,
underwear, suitcase etc. Seeing these objects above my head,
I noticed how impersonal they are and wondered how they influence
my subjectivity and art production.

Like the title *The Six Month Residency* implies, I packed the suitcase
for a six months stay. But it turned out that I lived with these objects
for almost a year due to different factors that seem common for
artists today. I once read that Bauhaus architects predicted that the
future 'man' would be flexible and wouldn't own a lot of stuff. They
designed new homes accordingly. Does a 'home' fit into a suitcase?

Supportive Measures Taken Prior To Incident
[Check All That Apply]:
☒ Increased level of observation
☒ Vivid cultural environment
☒ Artist integrated into the local art scene
☐ Professional group discussions
Motivation (mark appropriate):
|enthusiasm| obsession pleasure pain insomnia
|struggle||deadline| Other:

Cognitive Factors
[Check All That Apply]:
☒ Perception, attention
☐ Wondering
☐ Imagination, creativity
☒ Experimentation, play
☐ Planning, orientation
☐ Learning
☐ Memory
☐ Argumentation
☒ Introspection
☐ Extroversion
☐ Other:

Environment(s) In Which The Incident
Was Conceived And/Or Executed
[Answer with Yes or No]:
Studio **Yes**
Library **Yes**
Hardware store **Yes**
Workshops **No**
Space with adequate lighting **No**
Possibility for accommodation **Yes**

Acoustic environment (mark appropriate):
|Music| Noise Silence Other:
Cleanliness of environment (mark appropriate):
|Clean| Cluttered area Messy Other:
Recreational activities (mark appropriate):
|Dancing| Swimming Running Other:
Wifi (mark appropriate):
No connection Poor connection |Good connection|
Other:

Support
Name(s) And Function(s) Of The Person(s) Involved:
Christoph Pötsch, lent me his camera
Simone Etter, lent me her table
Petra Mrša, helped instal

Assistant's Advice was useful?
Needed More Advice That Was Not Available?
Advice Safely Used By Affected Artist(s)?
 Other:

Functional Factors
[Check All That Apply]:
☒ Desire
☐ Loneliness
☒ Connectedness
☐ Electricity
☐ Food
☐ Drinks
☒ Emotional balance
☐ Emotional unbalance
☐ Other:

Mobility
Position(s) taken (mark appropriate):
 sitting |standing| lying |moving| rolling

Body part(s) involved (mark appropriate):
|hands||fingers||arms||eyes|
 ears head |legs| mouth |toes|
 heart lungs hips Other:

Equipment Used To Manifest The Incident
[Check All That Apply]:
☐ Computer
☒ Chair
☐ Hot plate
☐ Camera
☐ Smartphone
☐ Projector
☐ Bicycle
☐ Bed
☒ Other:
Self-made construction to reach
the ceiling

Material Evidence With This Report
Mark Applicable Description(s) Of Accompanying
Material:

1st Page: Documentation |Installation view|
            Video Still Reproduction Other:

2nd Page: Documentation Installation view
            Video Still Reproduction Other:

3rd Page: Documentation Installation view
            Video Still Reproduction Other:

4th Page: Documentation Installation view
            Video Still Reproduction Other:

5th Page: Documentation Installation view
            Video Still Reproduction Other:

Completed by Gabriel Hensche   Signature:

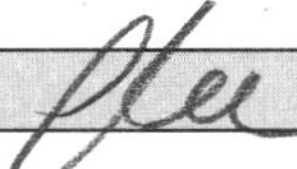

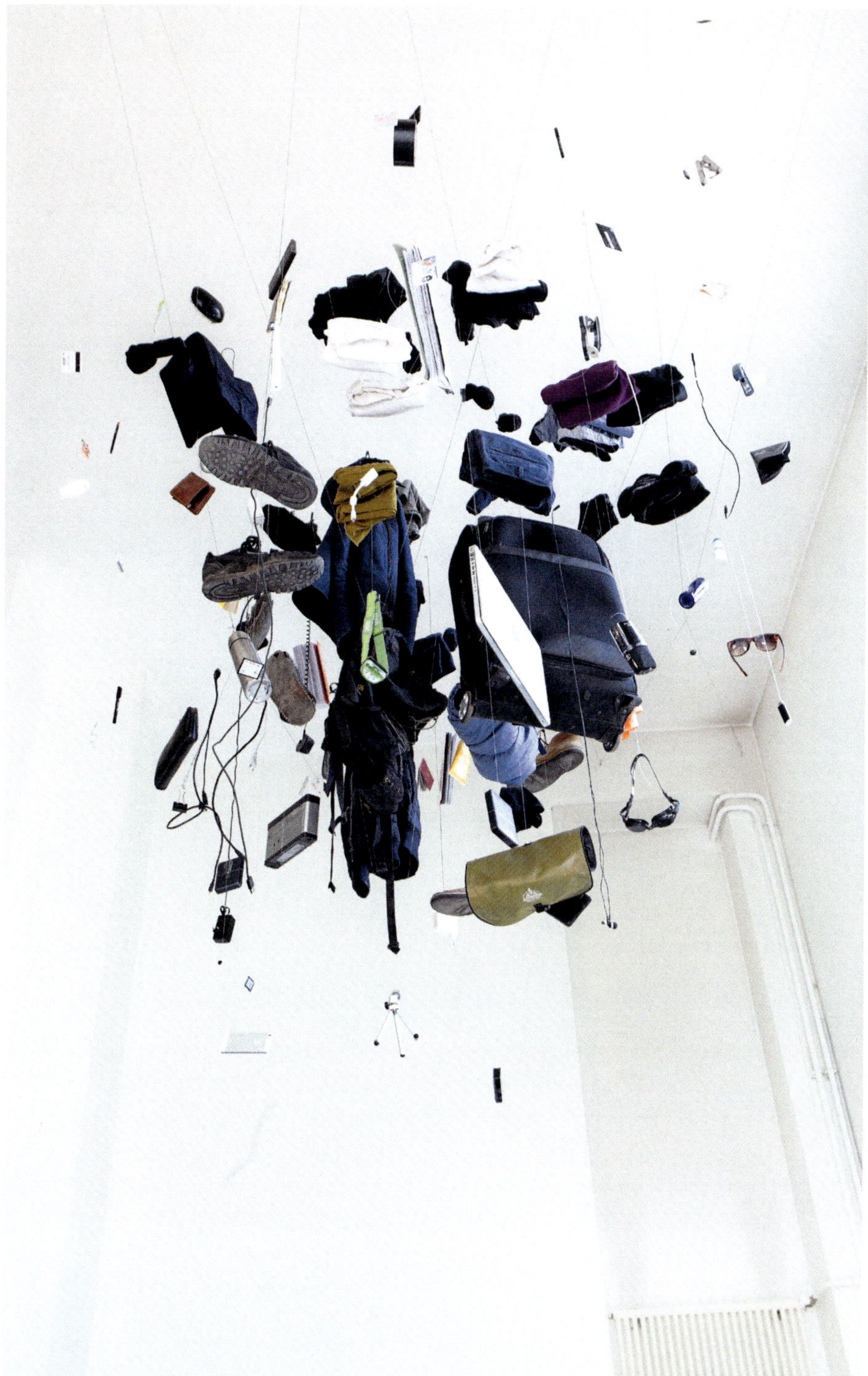

How to come at an incident when in fact you're stumbling onto the scene, cautiously entering in the middle and leaving before the end. Aware or unaware of how much of what you see is only a reflection of where you were mentally when you arrived; that your perception is only a mirror of yourself, your relationship concerns or economic fixations.

When watching a subject tumble down the stairs, begin to cry or marry another subject, our face may express a general reaction of joy, shock or excitement. Orally, we may support these general looks with specific observations about the occurrence. However, internally a movie has begun. We are observing our own relative experiences or predictions about possible futures, comparing and contrasting what we understand as leading to the scene before us and applying it to our own set, or possible set of events. We wonder at our own feelings if we were to become the subject or when we were them. As we grin and speak, this second dialogue is occurring; and if it is not heard in the voice of our third-eye deep within the coffers of our subconscious, it is felt like varying tonal reverberations within our chest—like a song we know well and to which our emotive response is familiar and ever-unchanged.

The approach of a mother to a child's closed door is similar, however with the addition of suspense and perhaps fear. The possible storylines may speed-up and overlap as she approaches the knob. Upon entering, her eyes may dart around the room looking for symbols, evidence or detritus. The first two are to support or undermine her predictions, and the third is to give her employment or purpose which in turn may provide her the relief that her presence has imprinted somehow on the space or narrative contained within.

A family photo placed on her desk, reminds her of the ideal she works toward with her everyday actions, which centre on togethering and fusing bonds. This image is only a distilled dream—of this she is aware. But like the chocolate bar she keeps in the drawer just below, it is a pleasure object, full of potential and short lived satisfaction. Should the figures in that image change would her feelings remain the same? She sometimes wonders. Do these people even know each other? How did they end up in this arrangement? What is it to be dedicated to a family (created or inherited) and how will she be sure when she's achieved it?

Incident Assessment & Investigation Findings:

I witnessed blindly coming to know the objects, elements or persons of Hensche's attention through temporary implosions of packed materials, in a suspended fall from the first to the second floor; all the while I recognized what I was seeing and that I didn't have the whole picture.

Quantum entanglements—of human and non-human matter—are a cluster of relations that further problematize the exclusive use of our tools of perception (mental, physical, mechanical) to identify singular meaning, persons, places or things. *I'm not sure,* but to the best of my knowledge entanglements are "a physical phenomenon which occurs when pairs or groups of particles are generated or interact in ways such that the quantum state of each particle cannot be described independently of the state of the other(s)…"[1] Each, therefore enter an impure-quantum condition by way of their entanglements; their characteristics blended in the dynamic exchange occurring between them and those pairs or groups generating within the same system.

By contrast, the more easily observable elements of one (particle) existing in a pure-quantum state (operating in solitude or autonomously) coupled with information about its inherent rules (or limitations), "exhaust" all possible predictions about its future behaviour. A kind of absolute understanding is attainable as a result of its consistent patterns, materials, environments or exchanges. Prediction is also possible with regard to quantum entanglements, however only if first we try to measure the interactions between particles in order that we may know in what ways they have become co-dependent, established hierarchies or routines. However, it is a fact that observing them changes their behaviour. Aware that they're being witnessed, they perform more or less; simpler or more complex actions as if to better communicate or confuse understanding of their intentions or restrictions. "As a result, some physicists do not give any physical reality to the concept of measurement or observation."[2] For them, the layered state of each particle does not allow one to clearly understand the individual or their production within entanglements, and the measured state, as recorded by the witness, does not really exist.

1   "Quantum entanglement", Wikipedia, https://en.wikipedia.org/wiki/Quantum_entanglement (accessed May 4, 2018).
2   "Schrödinger's cat", Wikipedia, https://en.wikipedia.org/wiki/Schrödinger%27s_cat (accessed, July 30, 2018).

Inextricable from each other, the who or what that is produced within an entanglement will not match the who or what that is produced at its fringes or beyond its borders. As something physical is not the same when made digital, the materials, habits, routines or meanings of ones production may cease after only hours on a *honeymoon in paradise.* If in such a place, errors in understanding each other are still occurring after: considerable analysis of outcomes (depth dependent on time), an *interview* and a *six month residency,* can schemas created during instances of pure-quantum activity correct present perceptions? Can subatomic intuition provide greater insight than what our eyes supply? Or are we lost to tools that cannot give us a unilateral expertise on shapes; stuck in an economy of knowledge that is simply the sum of collective perception?

Walking along a given path in surrounding jungles (urban or natural), the subtle sounds of bird song and the overhang of blue sky lead to questions about past, present and future possibilities, wonder about our presence on this planet, our existence together and the journeys we take knowingly or unknowingly with one another. Like *walking into our TV* there was a shimmer that told us this was someone else's reality. A set of tracks that looped depending on our position, gave only the semblance of here, and we too were recording our surroundings.

A honeymoon in paradise is an interesting setting because of its concentration of time and contact. It teeters on an ingrained cultural belief in its ability to solidify the union of two sides, such as an artist and their practice. Two sides which may have already been working and living together for years, may have developed habits, strategies and processes that help sustain their affection for and commitment to one another. Yet here at this juncture, I witnessed how the intensity of relative solitude unquestionably effected their relationship—for better or worse. Sometimes, after just committing, this 'time together' causes a split, an irrevocable frustration, or reveals unexpected differences. For others it re-invigorates the reasoning behind their collaboration. Introspection is unavoidable. The exaggerated pleasure of discussing the why and how of everything, of eating slowly, stretching more and reviewing ones possessions together, is conducive to it. The self, sprawled out over the floor of your impermanent home together—the interstitial space of your forever—is vulnerable—gratifyingly so. The material of one day is the waste of tomorrow, shifting on 24 hour cycles, productive becomes reductive until *the last one out turns off the lights.*